2 00

THE

MYSTERY

READER'S

QUIZ BOOK

ANETA CORSAUT
MUFF SINGER
ROBERT WAGNER

M. EVANS AND COMPANY, INC.
New York

Grateful acknowledgment is made to the following, for permission to reprint:

From *Blue Hammer*, by Ross MacDonald. © 1976 by Ross
MacDonald, Reprinted by permission of Alfred A. Knopf,
Inc.

From *Having a Wonderful Crime*, by Craig Rice. Reprinted by
permission of the author's Estate and the agents for the
Estate, Scott Meredith Literary Agency, 845 Third Avenue,
New York, N.Y. 10022.

From *The Long Lavendar Look*, by John D. MacDonald. © 1970
by John D. MacDonald. Reprinted by permission of Max
Wilkinson Associates.

From *The League of Frightened Men*, by Rex Stout. © 1935,
© renewed 1962 by Rex Stout. Reprinted by permission of
Viking Penguin, Inc.

0-87131-363-4   CLOTHBOUND

0-87131-351-0   PAPERBOUND

M. Evans and Company, Inc.
216 East 49 Street
New York, New York 10017

Design by RFS Graphic Design, Inc.

Manufactured in the United States of America

9 8 7 6 5 4 3 2 1

CONTENTS

To Rick Tuttle, Harry Singleton,
Goldryn Singer, Judy Singer, and
Paul Gillette
— accessories after the fact.
Thank you.

MAKING

THE CASE

If we err, therefore, in our liking of detective stories, we err with Plato.

—JOHN CARTER

We number some philistines among our friends who often express dismay at our interest in the curious world of crime fiction. They consider this pursuit not only a waste of time, but perhaps even evidence of arrested development.[1]

We like wending our way through mystery novels, where sense is made out of nonsense, unlike the real world, where too often the opposite seems to be the order of events.

A young man just returned from Russia was asked how the Russians feel about sex. "They like it," he replied. Not a bad answer, it seems to us. We like mysteries. We go on with our harmless amusement because we like it.

So to those who scoff and say, "Who cares whodunit?" we answer, "We do!" We not only care who, but to whom, and where, and when, and why—which is what this book is all about.

More and more people are joining us in the simple pleasures of the whodunit. Over the past few years there has been a steady increase in crime fiction readership.

FOOTPRINT

[1] We suspect many of these people of being closet mystery addicts.

Not only are mystery shelves lengthening in most bookstores, but several shops are dedicated exclusively to crime novels and mystery fiction. It's fun exchanging tidbits with like-minded readers as you browse.

We have found it interesting and entertaining to quiz each other on some of the vital facts contained within the world of mystery novels. This series of tests has been compiled for absolutely no useful purpose except our own enjoyment.[2] We hope that you will be entertained too.

These quizzes test you on many aspects of crime fiction. You will be asked not only who the "good guys" are, but also how they operate. Who helps or hinders them in crime solving? Where do they live? And, what sort of people are they?

We ask you to name villains, identify plots, and recognize authors by style and subject matter. Questions on mystery films and television detective stories are included, and we have added some questions about those authors we found especially interesting.

Above all, we have tried to keep this book entertaining as well as challenging. You will come across some old friends in these pages, and perhaps be encouraged to meet some new ones. We hope so.

This triviality is dedicated to all those who find Christie intriguing, Sayers fascinating, Hammett exciting, and MacDonald compelling.

"Come, Watson, the game's afoot."

FOOTPRINT

[2] Or did we do it for the money?

How to Reach a Verdict

No quiz book is complete without a way to check your know-how. There are two ways to rate yourself in The Mystery Reader's Quiz Book. As you finish each chapter, check your answers against the Solutions (starting on page 165) and total your point score to see how well you know each area in The Mystery Reader's Quiz Book.

At the end of the book, total your points from all the chapters. If you happen to rate in the master category, or close to it, go on to "Postmortems," the Master Sleuth's Quiz, which even we had trouble with.

So You Think You're a Fan

A good mystery novel is the answer to Lowell's question "What is so rare as a day in June . . ."

— FRANKLIN D. ROOSEVELT

Match the clues in the left column with the items in the right column. (Answers are below.) If you get at least half the answers right on this introductory quiz, you should not be completely at sea in the following pages. If you are close to half, then we recommend that you cheat. After all, you're not really being watched. Or are you?

_____	**1.** Agatha Christie	**A.** Baker Street
_____	**2.** Dick Francis	**B.** Asta
_____	**3.** Jack Webb	**C.** Roderick Alleyn
_____	**4.** Ross MacDonald	**D.** Philip Marlowe
_____	**5.** Nick and Nora Charles	**E.** Hercule Poirot
		F. *The Maltese Falcon*
_____	**6.** Mickey Spillane	**G.** Racetracks
_____	**7.** Sam Spade	**H.** Joe Friday
_____	**8.** Ngaio Marsh	**I.** Mike Hammer
_____	**9.** Raymond Chandler	**J.** Lew Archer
_____	**10.** Sherlock Holmes	

1. E   2. G   3. H   4. J   5. B   6. I   7. F   8. C   9. D   10. A

POTPOURRI

... The reading of detective stories, like the smoking of pipes, and the flogging of trout streams, becomes in a flash one of the outward signs of respectability ...

— TIMES LITERARY SUPPLEMENT
(FEBRUARY 1955)

The following potpourri reflects some of the variety of mystery memorabilia found on our own bookshelves, a sampling of writers, suspects, victims, and scenes of the crime. Perhaps you will catch up with some of your own favorites on this gallop across the broad landscape of detective fiction.

AUTHORS AND TITLES

Match the titles on the left with the authors on the right.
Score 2 points for each correct answer.

_____ 1. *Gaudy Night*   **A.** Agatha Christie

_____ 2. *Flying Finish*   **B.** Ethel Lina White

_____ 3. *Toward Zero*   **C.** Ross MacDonald

_____ 4. *The Lady*   **D.** Dorothy Sayers
         Vanishes
                                E. Dick Francis
_____ 5. *The Drowning*
         Pool

MYSTERY MINUTIAE

Score 3 points for each correct answer.

1. Which of the following people, through the device of
   the mystery story, sets out a theory to exonerate King
   Richard III of the murder of his two nephews in the
   Tower of London?

   _____ **A.** Mickey Spillane

   _____ **B.** Herbert Marshall

   _____ **C.** Josephine Tey

   _____ **D.** Mary Wollstonecraft Shelley

2. Along with mystery writing, Dame Ngaio Marsh has another interest. She wrote one of the following crime novels, which highlights this other interest. Which book is it?

_____ **A.** *Alibi Innings*

_____ **B.** *Murder in the Surgery*

_____ **C.** *Final Curtain*

_____ **D.** *On Her Majesty's Secret Service*

3. *The Encyclopedia of Mystery and Detection* (Steinbrunner and Penzler, 1976) notes that G. K. Chesterton's Father Brown has a first name. That name is mentioned twice, and only twice, in all fifty-one Father Brown stories. What is Father Brown's first name?

_____ **A.** Matthew

_____ **B.** Mark

_____ **C.** Luke

_____ **D.** Paul

4. Nicholas Freeling has created a sleuth with a sharp and penetrating eye for both the social and historical milieu. Who is this Inspector?

_____ **A.** Wilfred Dover

_____ **B.** Percy Faith

_____ **C.** Piet Van der Valk

_____ **D.** John Denson

5. In *Easy to Kill* by Agatha Christie, an elderly woman, similar to Jane Marple, helps solve the mystery. Can you identify her?

_____ **A.** Tuppence Beresford

_____ **B.** Lavinia Fullerton

_____ **C.** Margaret Rutherford

_____ **D.** Maud Silver

6. Identify the series detective created by Ruth Rendell.

_____ **A.** Alistair Sim

_____ **B.** Commissioner of Police John Appleby

_____ **C.** Chief Inspector Wexford

_____ **D.** Inspector McKee

7. Dashiell Hammett wrote a book about a retired private investigator. The book later became the basis for a popular MGM film series. Name the book.

_____ **A.** *The Thin Man*

_____ **B.** *Unnatural Causes*

_____ **C.** *That's Entertainment Part II*

_____ **D.** *Alibi for a Witch*

8. Nuri bey is the gentle detective in the book *Nothing Is the Number When You Die* by Joan Fleming. What is Nuri bey's nationality and occupation?

_____ **A.** Japanese car manufacturer

_____ **B.** Egyptian pilot

_____ **C.** Turkish scholar

_____ **D.** Greek magnate

9. Pam and Jerry are a famous detective husband-and-wife team. They are enjoyed as much for their zany wit as for their sleuthing. Can you identify them?

_____ **A.** Mr. and Mrs. Purbright

_____ **B.** Mr. and Mrs. Charles

_____ **C.** Mr. and Mrs. Bryce

_____ **D.** Mr. and Mrs. North

10. *The Devil Was Handsome* is the title of a book in which Chief Inspector Martineau of the Granchester Police appears. Who is the creator of Chief Inspector Martineau?

_____ **A.** Colin Watson

_____ **B.** Sax Rohmer

_____ **C.** Maurice Procter

_____ **D.** Detective Inspector C. D. Sloan

AUTHORS AND THEIR CHARACTERS

Match the authors on the left with the characters they created on the right. Score 2 points for each correct answer.

_____ 1. Harry Kemelman

_____ 2. Patricia Wentworth

_____ 3. Nicholas Blake

_____ 4. Rex Stout

_____ 5. John D. MacDonald

_____ 6. John Dickson Carr

_____ 7. Dashiell Hammett

_____ 8. Carolyn Wells

_____ 9. P. D. James

_____ 10. Simon Harvester

A. Nigel Strangeways

B. Travis McGee

C. Fleming Stone

D. Sam Spade

E. Adam Dalgliesh

F. Rabbi David Small

G. Dorian Silk

H. Maud Silver

I. Dr. Gideon Fell

J. Nero Wolfe

DON'T BUY A BOOK BY ITS COVER

Have you ever had the highly frustrating experience of buying a book by a favorite author, only to discover you'd already read it under another title? The following quiz focuses on alternate titles used by Agatha Christie, and should prove of some help to you and other Christie mystery fans on your next trip to the bookstore. Score 6 points for each correct match.

_____ 1. *Murder in Retrospect*

_____ 2. *Remembered Death*

_____ 3. *What Mrs. McGillicuddy Saw*

_____ 4. *Easy to Kill*

_____ 5. *Murder on the Orient Express*

_____ 6. *The Boomerang Clue*

_____ 7. *Thirteen at Dinner*

_____ 8. *So Many Steps to Death*

_____ 9. *Dead Man's Mirror*

_____ 10. *The Tuesday Club Murders*

A. *The Thirteen Problems*

B. *Murder in the Mews*

C. *Destination Unknown*

D. *Lord Edgeware Dies*

E. *Why Didn't They Ask Evans?*

F. *Murder in the Calais Coach*

G. *Murder Is Easy*

H. *4:50 from Paddington*

I. *Sparkling Cyanide*

J. *Five Little Pigs*

FREE ASSOCIATIONS

Match the clues on the left with the items on the right.
Score 2 points for each correct answer.

_____	**1.** Colonel Mustard	**A.** 87th Precinct
_____	**2.** Miss Marple	**B.** W. J. Burley
_____	**3.** Orchids	**C.** Miss Scarlet
_____	**4.** Lord Peter Wimsey	**D.** Brasserie Dauphine
_____	**5.** George and Bess	**E.** Margaret Rutherford
_____	**6.** Jules Maigret	**F.** Number One Son
_____	**7.** Perry Mason	**G.** Nero Wolfe
_____	**8.** Charlie Chan	**H.** Della Street
_____	**9.** Ed McBain	**I.** Nancy Drew
_____	**10.** Superintendent Wycliffe	**J.** Monocle

ELEMENTARY QUESTIONS

Score 3 points for each correct answer.

1. The creator of C. Auguste Dupin is generally known as the father of the detective story. Who is he?

_____ **A.** Wilkie Collins

_____ **B.** Edgar Allan Poe

_____ **C.** Mark Twain

_____ **D.** Robert Louis Stevenson

2. Which of the following supersleuths is not a lawyer?

_____ **A.** Perry Mason

_____ **B.** Mr. Tutt

_____ **C.** Ellery Queen

_____ **D.** Anthony Maitland

3. What is a master cracksman?

_____ **A.** Sharpshooter

_____ **B.** Safecracker

_____ **C.** Joke teller

_____ **D.** Bricklayer

4. Jimmy Stewart and Grace Kelly starred in a 1954 Paramount film from a short story called "It Had to be Murder" by Cornell Woolrich. What is the name of the film?

_____ **A.** _Rear Window_

_____ **B.** _How Green Was My Valley_

_____ **C.** _Psycho_

_____ **D.** _The Big Sleep_

5. Which of the following sleuths is not overweight?

_____ **A.** Nero Wolfe

_____ **B.** Jules Maigret

_____ **C.** Gideon Fell

_____ **D.** Charlie Chan

_____ **E.** Chief Inspector Hazelrigg

_____ **F.** They'd all better watch their weight.

6. Which of the following female sleuths is not a senior citizen?

_____ **A.** Miss Seeton

_____ **B.** Modesty Blaise

_____ **C.** Lavinia Fullerton

_____ **D.** Hildegarde Withers

_____ **E.** Mrs. Pollifax

7. *The Woman in White* and *The Moonstone* were written in the 1860s by which of the following authors?

_____ **A.** Louisa May Alcott

_____ **B.** Wilkie Collins

_____ **C.** Horace Walpole

_____ **D.** Mary Lincoln

8. Which of the following books was not written by Raymond Chandler?

_____ **A.** *The Smell of Fear*

_____ **B.** *The Three Coffins*

_____ **C.** *The Long Goodbye*

_____ **D.** *Farewell, My Lovely*

9. Mark McShane, who wrote *Séance on a Wet Afternoon,* has a penchant for elaborate titles. Which of the following titles is not by Mark McShane?

_____ **A.** *Ill Met at a Fish Market on George Street*

_____ **B.** *The Singular Case of the Multiple Dead*

_____ **C.** *The Querulous Knight of the Quarter Horse*

_____ **D.** None of the above are by Mark McShane.

10. Choose the detective who would *not* search the embers in the fireplace for charred letters, root through dustbins for the bloody handkerchief, or crawl about on all fours looking for clues in pursuit of whodunit.

_____ **A.** Lord Peter Wimsey

_____ **B.** Dr. Dollent

_____ **C.** Inspector Purbright

_____ **D.** Hercule Poirot

11. Which of the following authors would not let his or her victims be caught dead in a cozy manor house?

_____ **A.** Elizabeth Lemarchand

_____ **B.** Georgette Heyer

_____ **C.** Dick Francis

_____ **D.** Nicholas Blake

12. Which of the following authors created the mystery detective known as The Toff?

_____ **A.** John Creasey

_____ **B.** John Dickson Carr

_____ **C.** John D. MacDonald

_____ **D.** John Quincy Adams

13. What do the initials CID represent?

_____ **A.** Cops Investigating Disasters

_____ **B.** Cops In Disguise

_____ **C.** Criminal Investigation Department

_____ **D.** Criminus Interditus Detente

14. Which of the following is *not* an Arthur Conan Doyle book about Sherlock Holmes?

_____ **A.** *The Sign of the Four*

_____ **B.** *The Hound of the Baskervilles*

_____ **C.** *Valley of Fear*

_____ **D.** *Malice Aforethought*

15. Who created the short story detective hero Parker Pyne?

_____ **A.** Tucker Coe

_____ **B.** Agatha Christie

_____ **C.** Margaret Millar

_____ **D.** Julian Symons

16. What single word is missing from *Kidnap* _____ by Arthur B. Reeve and *The Hellfire* _____ by Donald Zochert?

_____ **A.** *Victim*

_____ **B.** *Plot*

_____ **C.** *Club*

_____ **D.** *Gang*

17. Which of the following mystery writers has written the most detective fiction novels?

_____ **A.** Dorothy Sayers

_____ **B.** John Creasey

_____ **C.** Dashiell Hammett

_____ **D.** Agatha Christie

18. If you plan to murder someone by serving deadly mushrooms, you choose the ones with the tiny white gills and wartlike marks.   True or False?

19. Little Caesar's name was Rico.   True or False?

20. Inspector Jules Maigret is a bachelor.   True or False?

JUST THE FACTS, MA'AM

Fill in the blanks and score 6 points for every correct answer.

1. Sam Spade, one of the best-known detectives, appears in only one full-length mystery novel. Name it.

2. Who is the detective featured in the colorful mystery adventures *The Deep Blue Good-by, The Long Lavender Look,* and *The Turquoise Lament?*

3. What award is presented each year at the Mystery Writers of America dinner in New York City?

4. Which detective sleuth has a popular mystery story magazine named after him?

5. What poet is Maud Silver, spinster enquiry agent, fond of quoting?

6. About which famous literary detective is Nicholas Meyer's *The Seven Per-Cent Solution?*

_____

7. What Scotland Yard detective has a flair for intuitive detection and often says "My nose tells me . . ."?

_____

8. Name the popular sleuth featured in the films *The Penguin Pool Murder, Murder on the Blackboard,* and *Murder on a Bridle Path.*

_____

9. Name Sherlock Holmes's smarter, younger brother.

_____

10. Which Theodore Dreiser novel is based on an actual crime?

_____

TELLING DETAILS

Score 3 points for each correct answer.

1. Which of the following crime novels is not by Earl Derr Biggers?

   _____ **A.** *The House Without a Key*

   _____ **B.** *The Chinese Parrot*

   _____ **C.** *Charlie Chan Carries On*

   _____ **D.** *Diamonds Are Forever*

2. Who is the detective hero featured in *Murder by the Book, Black Orchids, The Doorbell Rang,* and *Corsage?*

   _____ **A.** Nero Wolfe

   _____ **B.** Mike Hammer

   _____ **C.** Nick Charles

   _____ **D.** Mr. Moto

3. Who played the heroine in the series *Perils of Pauline?*

   _____ **A.** Mrs. Pym

   _____ **B.** Honey West

   _____ **C.** Pearl White

   _____ **D.** Christie Opara

4. Who wrote *Death of a Fool* and *Death of a Peer?*

_____ **A.** Ngaio Marsh

_____ **B.** John P. Marquand

_____ **C.** Sax Rohmer

_____ **D.** Ruth Rendell

5. Who created the sleuth Francis Quarles?

_____ **A.** Josephine Tey

_____ **B.** Julian Symons

_____ **C.** Frances and Richard Lockridge

_____ **D.** Edmond Crispin

6. John Rhode has created a clever amateur sleuth who teaches mathematics in between solving crimes. Name the sleuth.

_____ **A.** Dr. Lancelot Priestly

_____ **B.** Dr. Zhivago

_____ **C.** Professor Gervase Fen

_____ **D.** Dr. Reggie Fortune

7. Which of the following books was not written by Margery Allingham?

_____ **A.** *Traitor's Purse*

_____ **B.** *The Moving Toyshop*

_____ **C.** *Mind Readers*

_____ **D.** *Police at the Funeral*

8. Which of the following cases did Philo Vance solve?

_____ **A.** *The Case of the Seven Sneezes*

_____ **B.** *The Poisoned Chocolates Case*

_____ **C.** *The Gracie Allen Murder Case*

_____ **D.** *The Case of the Worried Waitress*

9. Which of the following police procedurals was not written by Ed McBain?

_____ **A.** *Killer's Choice*

_____ **B.** *Killer's Payoff*

_____ **C.** *Killer's Wedge*

_____ **D.** *Killer Bees*

10. Who wrote *Black Angel, Black Curtain, Black Path of Fear,* and *The Bride Wore Black?*

_____ **A.** Cornell Woolrich

_____ **B.** Helen Reilly

_____ **C.** Anthony Boucher

_____ **D.** Catherine Aird

THE LINGO

Match the crime lingo on the left with the definition on the right and indicate whether the jargon is American (A) or British (B) in origin. Score 2 points for each correct match, and 2 for each correct national origin.

_____ 1. Gunsel

_____ 2. Gumshoe

_____ 3. Nick

_____ 4. Whiz kid

_____ 5. Collar

_____ 6. Yellow sheet

_____ 7. Floater

_____ 8. Ripper

_____ 9. Brothel creepers

_____ 10. Wopsie

_____ 11. Murphy man

_____ 12. Heater

_____ 13. Hook

_____ 14. Handler

_____ 15. Loid

_____ 16. Mouthpiece

_____ 17. Baby-sitter

_____ 18. Cosh

A. Arrest
B. Policewoman
C. Soft-soled shoes
D. Lawyer
E. Rapidly promoted police officer
F. Telephone bugging equipment
G. Con man
H. Safecracker
I. Contract killer, assassin
J. Body pulled from a body of water
K. Detective or policeman
L. Record of past arrests
M. Plastic, particularly a credit card
N. Weighted weapon similar to a black-jack
O. Powerful friend— with influence
P. Police station
Q. Gun
R. Receiver of stolen merchandise

A FEW CROSS WORDS

Score 75 points for completing the puzzle.

1		2		3			4		5				6
7							8				9		
				10		11							
12						13							
					14				15	16		17	
18		19					20				21		
						22			23				
24		25							26				
			27			28							
		29		30	31				32				
							33	34					
35													

ACROSS

1 Harriet and Peter owe their lives to her
7 Prisoner serving the maximum sentence
8 Joan Fleming's _____ *Is the Number When You Die*
10 A ruffian or hood
12 Montague Egg's line of work
13 Grabs or arrests
15 Raffles's livelihood

18 Nicholas Freeling's love in what Western European city?

21 _____ *Bertram's Hotel*

22 Asey Mayo was known as "The _____ Sherlock"

24 Helen Reilly's _____ *Your Poison*

26 London art museum

27 Pronoun

28 Patrick Grant's profession

29 Successful punch (abbrev.)

30 What Duncan Maclain can't do

32 The Lone Wolf by another name

33 Dalgliesh might write one

35 Book in which Patricia Wentworth's butler stabbed the victim with the help of an elephant

DOWN

1 AKA Ethel Linnington

2 British gentleman-thief

3 Perry Mason's definition of wrongful civil acts

4 Warren Kiefer's '72 Edgar winner

5 Agather Troy's profession

6 The _____ _____ _____ _____, Sherlock's second case

9 _____ *The Heat of the Night*

11 First two initials of the host in *Ten Little Indians*

14 _____ *Last Case*

16 Dr. Fell, Nero Wolfe, and Maigret have this in abundance

17 Creasey's "Handsome"—from the opposite direction

19 Ngaio Marsh's *Death in a White* _____

20 The procedure (abbrev.)

23 Desdemona's downfall

25 Helen Reilly's dour cop

31 Auricle

32 A gumshoe does this kind of work

33 _____ *of Death* by Agatha Christie (abbrev.)

34 *Mr.* _____, a prosecuting sleuth (abbrev.)

SCORING

Authors and Titles	_____
Mystery Minutiae	_____
Authors and Their Characters	_____
Don't Buy A Book By Its Cover	_____
Free Associations	_____
Elementary Questions	_____
Just the Facts, Ma'am	_____
Telling Details	_____
The Lingo	_____
A Few Cross Words	_____
Chapter Total Score	_____

The Verdict

If you scored between 437 and 291
Hooray! You're off to a great start and obviously know (and love) your mysteries.

If you scored between 290 and 145
Well ... we caught you napping a few times, but you have the makings of a real fan.

If you scored between 144 and 0
Hey! Reading in bed is all well and good, but try staying awake now and then.

ABOUT

THE

GOOD GUYS

Clearly there could be no detective stories until
there are detectives....

— HOWARD HAYCRAFT

With all due apologies to literary creations such as the antihero and nonhero, we still like mystery stories with just plain heroes. Certainly most of the successful writers of whodunits have created heroes and heroines of wide audience appeal.

Some fictional detectives—private and public—can be compared to the knight-errant or the rugged individualist. Lew Archer and Philip Marlowe go it alone, doggedly pursue truth, and remain incorruptible in a world full of con men, crooked cops, and dishonest clients.

Jane Marple and Lord Peter Wimsey are equally appealing, although far more respectable.

From the cop on the beat to the had-I-but-known heroine menaced by dark secrets, we can choose a sleuth to suit our whim. We three have each discovered our own particular favorites, whom we have come to know as friends.

This chapter will test you on the good guys. You will have to know more than just who they are and who created them—the styles, hobbies, and idiosyncrasies of detective heroes are what we are concerned with in the following questions.

FITTING THE DESCRIPTION

Use your wits to match the detective with the appropriate description. Score 3 points for each correct answer.

1. Nancy Drew
2. Simon Templar, the Saint
3. Martin Beck
4. Philip Marlowe
5. Nick Charles
6. Albert Campion
7. Hercule Poirot
8. Sir Henry Merrivale
9. John Appleby
10. Sam Spade
11. Roderick Alleyn
12. Maud Silver

_____ **A.** His nickname is Rory or "Handsome," and he has been described as a mix between a grandee and a monk.

_____ **B.** This sleuth is Cambridge-educated, fair-haired, and quite thin. He sometimes speaks in a silly falsetto voice, while peering foolishly through large glasses. He is smarter than he looks.

_____ **C.** Michael Innes's charming and erudite sleuth married into an eccentric family. He is fond of literary allusion, and is knighted during his brilliant career.

_____ **D.** Blond and slim, this detective solves mysteries with good chums George and Bess.

_____ **E.** He is a rotund, bald man who performs magic tricks and loves to shout obscenities. Surprisingly, he lives up to his boast that he can do anything.

_____ **F.** This sleuth is good-looking, athletic, and fluent in several languages. He is a modern-day Robin Hood who always leaves a calling card.

_____ **G.** He is a famous man-about-town who changed his name from Charalambides. He has a dog, and a rich wife.

_____ **H.** San Francisco is home ("my burg") to this hard-boiled but idealistic detective, who often breaks the law and tangles with gunsels.

_____ **I.** This Los Angeles-based detective ("Trouble is my business") loves chess, is college-educated, and is fiercely loyal to his clients.

_____ **J.** She is a former governess, and a spinster who loves to knit. She has a penchant for wearing dowdy hats.

_____ **K.** This head of the Stockholm Homicide Squad smokes incessantly and has an unhappy marriage.

_____ **L.** He is vain, waxes his mustache, dyes his hair, and dresses like a dandy. Upon his retirement he takes to gardening, but still meticulously solves crimes.

SUPERSLEUTHS

Score 3 points for each correct response.

1. Which of the following heroes often tracked political enemies of England?

   _____ **A.** Arsène Lupin

   _____ **B.** Bulldog Drummond

   _____ **C.** Inspector Napoleon Bonaparte

   _____ **D.** Nicholas Freeling

2. Lord Peter Wimsey once had a love affair with which one of the following?

   _____ **A.** A Viennese opera singer

   _____ **B.** An American nurse

   _____ **C.** A minister of transportation

   _____ **D.** Margery Allingham

3. Sir Henry Merrivale is a favorite character of which famous author?

   _____ **A.** Caroline Keene

   _____ **B.** Carter Dickson

   _____ **C.** Eric Ambler

   _____ **D.** Orson Welles

4. The dour Inspector McKee of Centre Street was created by which of the following authors?

_____ **A.** Helen Reilly

_____ **B.** William Bendix

_____ **C.** Leslie Ford

_____ **D.** John Creasey

5. Pick the professional mystery writer-detective noted for his absentmindedness and his fine collection of rare books.

_____ **A.** Stanton Forbes

_____ **B.** Samuel Pepys

_____ **C.** Ellery Queen

_____ **D.** Superintendent Tibbit

6. Phoebe Atwood Taylor created the beloved "Cape Cod Sherlock." Who is he?

_____ **A.** Asey Mayo

_____ **B.** Cabot Atwood Lodge

_____ **C.** Taylor Cabot Lodge

_____ **D.** Professor Henry Poggioli

7. Josephine Tey's elegant Scotland Yard inspector is on sick leave in two of her novels. Who is he?

_____ **A.** Philip Trent

_____ **B.** Virgil Tibbs

_____ **C.** Alan Grant

_____ **D.** Anthony Trent

8. Which detective is a mystery novel fan?

_____ **A.** Sam Spade

_____ **B.** Ivor Maddox

_____ **C.** Mr. Moto

_____ **D.** Wilfred Dover

9. Leslie Ford, writing under the pseudonym of David Frome, created a timid widower who loves movies and works on cases with Inspector J. Humphrey Bull. Who is he?

_____ **A.** Michael Shayne

_____ **B.** Gervase Fen

_____ **C.** Evan Pinkerton

_____ **D.** Charles Lamb

10. Nurse Sarah Keate and Lance O'Leary work together in Mignon G. Eberhart's mysteries. What is Lance's profession?

_____ **A.** Mortician

_____ **B.** Doctor

_____ **C.** Mystery writer

_____ **D.** Police officer

11. Ian Carmichael played a famous sleuth in a 1973 BBC series set in 1920s England. Who is the highly intelligent and eccentric sleuth?

_____ **A.** Henry Gamadge

_____ **B.** Superintendent Folly

_____ **C.** Peter Wimsey

_____ **D.** Charles Laughton

12. Which of the following sleuths had a volume of poetry published?

　_____ **A.** Adam Dalgliesh

　_____ **B.** Lieutenant Richard Tuck

　_____ **C.** Miss Seeton

　_____ **D.** Ellery Queen

13. Which of the following detectives is most often sneezing and sniffling from a cold?

　_____ **A.** Father Brown

　_____ **B.** Perry Mason

　_____ **C.** Jules Maigret

　_____ **D.** Charlie Chan

14. Which of the following detective heroes limps?

　_____ **A.** Judge Dee

　_____ **B.** Philo Vance

　_____ **C.** James Bond

　_____ **D.** Anthony Gethryn

15. Who is the sleuth in *An Unsuitable Job for a Woman?*

　_____ **A.** Cordelia Gray

　_____ **B.** Modesty Blaise

　_____ **C.** Gypsy Rose Lee

　_____ **D.** Kate Fansler

IT'S A LIVING

Most people have to earn a living one way or another. Some detect, either privately or for a public agency. In crime fiction virtually every manner of professional detective is represented. However, there is still plenty of crime left over for the amateur.

Mark A for Amateur or P for Professional next to each of the following sleuths. Whether or not the detective charges a fee or is paid a salary is the criterion. Score 2 points for each positive identification.

_____ **1.** Ellery Queen

_____ **2.** Philo Vance

_____ **3.** Andrew Dalziel

_____ **4.** Lord Peter Wimsey

_____ **5.** Joseph French

_____ **6.** Hildegarde Withers

_____ **7.** The Mod Squad

_____ **8.** Dr. Basil Willing

_____ **9.** The Continental Op

_____ **10.** David Small

_____ **11.** Patrick Grant

_____ **12.** Nigel Strangeways

_____ **13.** Ira Cobb

_____ **14.** Drury Lane

_____ **15.** Ghanesh Ghote

_____ **16.** Nancy Drew

_____ **17.** Michael Shayne

_____ **18.** Adam Dalgliesh

_____ **19.** George Gideon

_____ **20.** Jules Maigret

BRITISH AND AMERICANS

The British sleuth, no matter how busy, takes time for tea or ale at the pub. His American cousin probably grabs a cup of coffee or a beer at a roadside cafe. What they wear, how they talk, and even the nature of the crime may differ depending on which side of the Atlantic our sleuth works.

Mark A for American or B for British next to the following sleuths. Score 2 points for each correct answer.

1. Albert Campion _____

2. Lew Archer _____

3. Eliot Ness _____

4. Inspector Hazelrigg _____

5. Mike Hammer _____

6. Dr. Gideon Fell _____

7. Montague Egg _____

8. Father Brown _____

9. Ellery Queen _____

10. Tim Corrigan _____

ACCESSORIES

Use the clues on the left to identify the detectives on the right. Score 3 points for each correct answer.

_____	1. "Brolly"	**A.** Maud Silver
_____	2. Volumes of obscure German poetry	**B.** Toussaint Moore
		C. George Smiley
_____	3. Cats	**D.** Lamont Cranston
_____	4. No. 33 rue Donot	**E.** Raffles
_____	5. Sergeant Heath	**F.** Miss Emily Seeton
_____	6. Philip Youngman Carter	**G.** Albert Campion
		H. Philo Vance
_____	7. Bunny Manders	**I.** Arsène Lupin
_____	8. Knitting needles	**J.** Rachel Murdock
_____	9. Harlem	
_____	10. The Shadow	

MORE MINUTIAE

Score 4 points for each correct answer.

1. Inspector Napoleon Bonaparte of the Queensland, Australia, police inherited blue eyes from his father, brown skin from his aborigine mother, and one of the following nicknames from his friends.

_____ **A.** Bony

_____ **B.** Nappy

_____ **C.** Emperor

_____ **D.** Blue Eyes

2. The Honorable Richard Rollison is a handsome gentleman adventurer. His intrigues take him all over London. What is his nickname?

_____ **A.** Bunny

_____ **B.** The Toff

_____ **C.** Rolly

_____ **D.** Dicky

3. Superintendent Hannasyde and Inspector Hemingway were both created by a detective fiction writer who also wrote many historical novels about the Regency days in London. Who is this author?

_____ **A.** Elizabeth Lemarchand

_____ **B.** Margaret Yorke

_____ **C.** Graham Greene

_____ **D.** Georgette Heyer

4. What is the nickname of the Mary Roberts Rinehart nurse-sleuth, Hilda Adams?

_____ **A.** Miss Plumperton

_____ **B.** Miss Pinkerton

_____ **C.** Miss Tinkerbell

_____ **D.** Miss Susan Dare

5. Which of the following sleuths is Oxford-educated?

_____ **A.** Roger Sheringham

_____ **B.** Albert Campion

_____ **C.** Nero Wolfe

_____ **D.** Paul Temple

6. Hugh Pentecost's short French detective manages a luxury hotel. Name him.

_____ **A.** Matt Cobb

_____ **B.** Adam Dalgliesh

_____ **C.** Charles Paris

_____ **D.** Pierre Chambrun

7. Before embarking on his many crime-solving adventures, what was Sherlock Holmes's occupation?

_____ **A.** Beekeeper

_____ **B.** Male model

_____ **C.** Realtor

_____ **D.** Tour guide

8. Which of the following detectives is fond of cats and Zen?

_____ **A.** Travis McGee

_____ **B.** Nick Charles

_____ **C.** Rinus De Gier

_____ **D.** Mandrake the Magician

9. When not sidetracked from his professional responsibilities, John Putnam Thatcher is generally found in which of the following places?

_____ **A.** The Tenderloin district

_____ **B.** Wall Street

_____ **C.** Dodger Stadium

_____ **D.** The JPT Ranch

10. Which of the following detectives solves crimes in between seminars at St. Mark's College?

_____ **A.** Dr. Thorndyke

_____ **B.** Dr. Fu Manchu

_____ **C.** Dr. Patrick Grant

_____ **D.** Dr. Reggie Fortune

11. Phoebe Atwood Taylor's tobacco-chewing detective once earned his living as which of the following?

_____ **A.** Sailor

_____ **B.** Tobacconist

_____ **C.** Epicene

_____ **D.** Mystery writer

12. Modesty Blaise, female detective, first arrives on the scene in which of the following?

_____ **A.** The novel *Shilling for Candles*

_____ **B.** A United Kingdom comic strip

_____ **C.** The film *Dial M for Murder*

_____ **D.** The TV series *Kojak*

13. Which of the following detectives is Belgian-born?

_____ **A.** Georges Simenon

_____ **B.** Gabriel Hanaud

_____ **C.** Hercule Poirot

_____ **D.** Moses Wine

14. Which of the following detectives has more than his fair share of hysterical females for clients?

_____ **A.** Father Brown

_____ **B.** Commander George Gideon

_____ **C.** Travis McGee

_____ **D.** Inspector Ganesh Ghote

15. Josephine Tey's detective Allen Grant makes his first appearance in which of the following mystery novels?

_____ **A.** *The Man in the Cue*

_____ **B.** *The Documents in the Case*

_____ **C.** *The Talented Mr. Ripley*

_____ **D.** *Murders in Praed Street*

16. Which detective solves *The Mystery Of Marie Roget?*

_____ **A.** Maurice Le Blanc

_____ **B.** C. Auguste Dupin

_____ **C.** Maurice Chevalier

_____ **D.** Augustus Mandrell

17. Which detective is featured in *Stopover Tokyo?*

_____ **A.** William Holden

_____ **B.** Evan Pinkerton

_____ **C.** Dr. Thorndyke

_____ **D.** Mr. Moto

18. Which hero frequently solves a case by overhearing the nefarious plans of the crooks and then physically confronting them?

_____ **A.** Philip Marlowe

_____ **B.** Ellery Queen

_____ **C.** Bulldog Drummond

_____ **D.** Mrs. Pollifax

19. Which detective is handsome, well groomed, confident, and blind?

_____ **A.** Captain Duncan Maclain

_____ **B.** Casey Flashgun

_____ **C.** Scarlet Pimpernel

_____ **D.** Dr. Grace Severance

20. What famous sleuth dies in the book *Curtain?*

_____ **A.** Modesty Blaise

_____ **B.** Jane Marple

_____ **C.** Roderick Alleyn

_____ **D.** Hercule Poirot

ADMISSIBLE EVIDENCE

Match the clues on the left with the sleuths on the right.
Score 4 points for each correct answer.

_____ **1.** Polly Burton

_____ **2.** *The Doomdorf Mystery*

_____ **3.** Green spectacles

_____ **4.** Boulevard Richard Lenoir

_____ **5.** *An Unsuitable Job for a Woman*

_____ **6.** Blind

_____ **7.** Foreign cars

_____ **8.** 17 Richmond Street

_____ **9.** Professor of English

_____ **10.** *The Book of the Crime*

A. C. Auguste Dupin

B. Cordelia Gray

C. Max Carrados

D. Sergeant Luis Mendoza

E. Uncle Abner

F. Kate Fansler

G. Parker Pyne

H. The Old Man in the Corner

I. Henry Gamadge

J. Jules Maigret

GREAT GUMSHOES

Score 4 points for each correct answer.

1. What is television's well-known Chief Ironside's less well known first name?

    _____ **A.** Robert

    _____ **B.** Bessemer

    _____ **C.** Henry

    _____ **D.** Merrimac

2. George Harmon Coxe's sleuth Kent Murdoch earns his living at which of the following occupations?

    _____ **A.** Taking pictures for a newspaper

    _____ **B.** Driving a taxicab

    _____ **C.** Tap dancing

    _____ **D.** Clipping coupons

3. Superintendent turned Commander Gideon has which of the following nicknames?

    _____ **A.** J. J. Marric

    _____ **B.** The Reverend

    _____ **C.** The Boss

    _____ **D.** G. G.

4. Who is endearingly called the "revered preceptress" by a favorite police ally?

    _____ **A.** Christie Opara

    _____ **B.** Maud Silver

_____ **C.** Mrs. North

_____ **D.** Bertha Cool

5. *A Bullet for Midas* and *The Dear Dead Girls* by Nigel Morland feature which Deputy Assistant Commissioner of Scotland Yard?

_____ **A.** Tommy Rankin

_____ **B.** Cournacki

_____ **C.** Mrs. Pym

_____ **D.** Francis Pettigrew

6. Which sleuth created by Arthur B. Reeve is a Columbia University professor who uses psychoanalysis in crime solving? He has been referred to as "the American Sherlock Holmes."

_____ **A.** Colonel Braxton

_____ **B.** Mike Hammer

_____ **C.** Ira Cobb

_____ **D.** Craig Kennedy

7. When Sir Arthur Conan Doyle stopped writing Holmes stories, author August Derleth tried to keep Sherlock Holmes alive by creating which of the following sleuths, known as "the Sherlock Holmes of Praed Street"?

_____ **A.** Solar Pons

_____ **B.** Evan Pinkerton

_____ **C.** Mr. Chameleon

_____ **D.** Ian Firth

8. Which John Dickson Carr-created sleuth heads the Scotland Yard Department of Queer Complaints?

_____ **A.** Earl Drake

_____ **B.** Colonel March

_____ **C.** Anthony Gethryn

_____ **D.** Gay Stanhope

9. What is the most noticeable characteristic of good guy magazine writer Peter Styles?

_____ **A.** He is a dwarf.

_____ **B.** His hair is green.

_____ **C.** He has only one eye.

_____ **D.** He has only one leg.

10. Lawyer and amateur sleuth Francis Pettigrew was created by which of the following mystery novelists?

_____ **A.** Ted White

_____ **B.** Patricia Wentworth

_____ **C.** Cyril Hare

_____ **D.** Alan Hunter

THE TRUTH WILL OUT

Score 3 points for each correct answer.

1. Charlie Chan's last recorded case is _Keeper of the Keys._ True or False?

2. Sleuth Bernie Simmons of the New York District Attorney's office was created by Richard Lockridge. True or False?

3. Bulldog Drummond cracked *The Kennel Murder Case.* True or False?

4. Mr. Moto is featured in *The Dragon Murder Case.* True or False?

5. *Sabre Tooth, The Impossible Virgin,* and *Pieces of Modesty* feature Modesty Blaise. True or False?

6. Ellery Queen is the crime solver in *Blind Man's Bluff* and *Blind Alley.* True or False?

7. Inspector Ganesh Ghote solves the mystery of *The Perfect Murder.* True or False?

8. Mickey Spillane's *Bloody Sunrise* and *The Death of Dealers* feature hard-boiled Tiger Mann in the role of hero. True or False?

9. In the book *Roseanna,* Inspector Napoleon Bonaparte of the Queensland Police investigates the murder of an American whose body is found in a Swedish canal. True or False?

10. Amateur sleuth Roger Sheringham comes up with the wrong solution in *The Poisoned Chocolates Case,* but all ends well. True or False?

11. Tommy Hambledon is the patriotic good guy with a penchant for espionage in *Dover One.* True or False?

12. Britt Reid, reportedly the grandnephew of the Lone Ranger, fights crime under the name of the Green Lantern. True or False?

13. Peter Duluth, created by Patrick Quentin, is practically an alcoholic in his first adventure, *A Puzzle for Fools,* but recovers to solve other mysteries in subsequent novels. True or False?

14. Sleuth Asey Mayo is sometimes called "the codfish Sherlock."   True or False?

15. The Falcon's first name is Happy.   True or False?

SCORING

Fitting the Description   _____

Supersleuths   _____

It's a Living   _____

British and Americans   _____

Accessories   _____

More Minutiae   _____

Admissible Evidence   _____

Great Gumshoes   _____

The Truth Will Out   _____

     Chapter Total Score   _____

The Verdict

If you scored between 376 and 251
You and Sherlock could probably go into business together.

If you scored between 250 and 125
Like Dr. Watson, you know a lot but you need the help of a Holmes.

If you scored between 124 and 0
As Philip Marlowe might say, "Go home, little sister, I'll handle this."

MORE

THAN

JUST FRIENDS—

Meet the Sidekicks

"This is my friend Dr. Watson. He has been of most vital use to me..."

> —SHERLOCK HOLMES
> from *The Man with the Twisted Lip*

The sidekick is an oft-used device in mystery fiction, for a variety of reasons. Watson is the narrator who provides us with clues and insights as the story unfolds. Inspector Jules Maigret relies on the special talents and expertise of Moers, a lab technician and graphologist par excellence. Sometimes authors create sidekicks who represent a different class of society from that of the major sleuth. Aristocrat Albert Campion gains valuable information through the underworld connections of his ex-convict butler.

Another conventional use for sidekicks is comedy, provided unintentionally by the bumbler or deliberately by the clever wit.

We like sidekicks because we think two sets of eyes are better than one.

"WATSON, STAND NEXT TO THE GUY WITH THE PIPE..."

Match the hero on the left with his sidekick on the right. Score 2 points for each correct answer.

_____	**1.** Roderick Alleyn	**A.** Bunter
_____	**2.** Lord Peter Wimsey	**B.** Archie Goodwin
_____	**3.** Chief Inspector Wexford	**C.** Paul Drake
_____	**4.** Nero Wolfe	**D.** Quancy
_____	**5.** Ivor Maddox	**E.** Jimmy Pride
_____	**6.** John Appleby	**F.** Cesar Rodriguez
_____	**7.** Inspector McKee	**G.** Mike Burden
_____	**8.** Perry Mason	**H.** Captain Hastings
_____	**9.** Hercule Poirot	**I.** Br'er Fox
_____	**10.** Drury Lane	**J.** Inspector Todhunter

UNLIKELY PARTNERSHIPS

Score 4 points for each correct answer.

1. Albert Campion's surly but lovable sidekick was once occupied as which of the following?

_____ **A.** A porter from Heathrow Airport

_____ **B.** An embezzler

_____ **C.** A burglar

_____ **D.** An epicene

2. One of Roderick Alleyn's associates is a journalist. His attempts to help Alleyn solve the crime are rarely successful. Who is he?

_____ **A.** Alfred Hitchcock

_____ **B.** Phineas T. Buck

_____ **C.** Nigel Bathgate

_____ **D.** T. H. Mencken

3. Before becoming a "gentleman's gentleman" to Lord Peter Wimsey, Bunter (maker of extraordinarily good coffee) had met and worked with Wimsey. Choose the correct circumstances.

_____ **A.** They were in the Great War together.

_____ **B.** They met at Cambridge, where Lord Peter was a student and Bunter was Wimsey's clerk.

_____ **C.** They were both volunteers at the local Anti-Vivisection Society.

_____ **D.** They met at a coffee plantation in South China and together solved *The Murder on the Orient Expresso.*

4. Djuna is an adolescent assistant to which of the following sleuths?

_____ **A.** Peter Duluth

_____ **B.** Ellery Queen

_____ **C.** Mr. Moto

_____ **D.** Mrs. Pym

5. Louis Carlyle, sidekick to sleuth Max Carrados, is which of the following?

_____ **A.** Defrocked priest

_____ **B.** Rehabilitated poisoner

_____ **C.** Former embezzler

_____ **D.** Disbarred solicitor

6. The solitary C. Auguste Dupin has a loyal friend who chronicles Dupin's cases. Who is this devoted assistant?

_____ **A.** Martian

_____ **B.** Le Chiffre

_____ **C.** Heather Angel

_____ **D.** The chronicler is anonymous.

7. Ariadne Oliver, the mystery-writing sidekick sleuth, appears as the lead detective in which of the following whodunits?

_____ **A.** _Curtain_

_____ **B.** _Murder at the Vicarage_

_____ **C.** _The Pale Horse_

_____ **D.** _I'm No Murderer_

8. Miss Alexandra Katherine Climpson runs an agency of maiden ladies who assist which of the following sleuths in crime detection?

_____ **A.** Lord Peter Wimsey

_____ **B.** Nigel Strangeways

_____ **C.** Mike Hammer

_____ **D.** Charlie Chan

9. Theodolinda (Dol) Bonner heads a detective agency that helps on cases of which of the following armchair detectives?

_____ **A.** Father Brown

_____ **B.** Sam Spade

_____ **C.** Nero Wolfe

_____ **D.** The Old Man in the Corner

10. Inspectors Lucas, Janvier, Lapointe, and Torrance are police assistants to which of the following criminal investigators?

_____ **A.** Arsène Lupin

_____ **B.** Piet Van der Valk

_____ **C.** Martin Beck

_____ **D.** Jules Maigret

WORKING WITH THEM OR AGAINST THEM

Some of our favorite private sleuths solve the mystery of whodunit with the help of a police ally. Other times, the case is solved *despite* the involvement of the professional police. The interaction—be it friendly or hostile rivalry—does enhance the plot. Match the supersleuths on the left with the officials on the right. Score 3 points for each correct answer.

_____	**1.** Merlini	**A.** Monsieur G___
_____	**2.** Nero Wolfe	**B.** Humbleby
_____	**3.** Maud Silver	**C.** Lestrade
_____	**4.** C. Auguste Dupin	**D.** District Attorney Burger
_____	**5.** Henry Gamadge	
_____	**6.** Gervase Fen	**E.** Henry Arnold
_____	**7.** Sherlock Holmes	**F.** Homer Gavigan
_____	**8.** Hercule Poirot	**G.** Japp
_____	**9.** Perry Mason	**H.** Frank Abbott
_____	**10.** Desmond Merrion	**I.** Nordhall
		J. Inspector Cramer

(**Note:** This chapter and the next are scored together.)

MUCH MORE

THAN

JUST FRIENDS—

Wives and Lovers

The less love in a detective story, the better.
  —DOROTHY L. SAYERS

The hard-boiled private eye may have affairs but he usually avoids permanent relationships. On the other hand, there are many professional and amateur detectives whose wives and lovers are very much a part of their lives. The list includes bright young couples and very married senior citizens.

Often the woman is a helpmate to our detective hero. Women hear gossip, they intuit, they observe—a fashion inconsistency, a reupholstered sofa—and there it is, the solution! Over toast and coffee, the vital clue is passed to the male sleuth.

In the hands of the best authors, women are always interesting and add much to our enjoyment of the mystery.

HIS AND HERS

Match the sleuth on the left with his spouse or lady friend on the right. Score 3 points for each correct answer.

_____ **1.** Nick Charles

_____ **2.** Perry Mason

_____ **3.** Colonel John Primrose

_____ **4.** Roderick Alleyn

_____ **5.** Albert Campion

_____ **6.** Lord Peter Wimsey

_____ **7.** John Appleby

_____ **8.** Antony Maitland

_____ **9.** Henry Gamadge

_____ **10.** Piet Van der Valk

A. Arlette

B. Judith Raven

C. Della Street

D. Troy

E. Grace Latham

F. Nora

G. Jenny

H. Clara

I. Amanda Fitten

J. Harriet Vane

THE BETTER HALF

Score 3 points for each correct answer.

1. Irene Adler was the only love of which famous good guy?

_____ **A.** Sherlock Holmes

_____ **B.** Charlie Chan

_____ **C.** Nero Wolfe

_____ **D.** Philo Vance

2. Judith Raven, a good guy's famous wife, carved out a career in her own right. Pick the correct profession.

_____ **A.** Novelist

_____ **B.** Ornithologist

_____ **C.** Sculptor

_____ **D.** Epicene

3. Detective Steve Carella has a beautiful deaf-mute wife in which of the following detective series?

_____ **A.** *Wilcox Avenue* by Elizabeth Linnington

_____ **B.** *87th Precinct* by Ed McBain

_____ **C.** *Mike Shayne* by Brett Halliday

_____ **D.** *Mr. and Mrs. North* by Frances and Richard Lockridge

4. Choose the artist from the following well-known wives.

_____ **A.** Agather Troy

_____ **B.** Elaine Wagstaff

_____ **C.** Helene Justus

_____ **D.** Nora Charles

5. Lady Amanda Fitten was especially interested in which of the following?

_____ **A.** Tennis

_____ **B.** Astronomy

_____ **C.** Aero-Engineering

_____ **D.** Astrology

6. Harriet Vane first meets her husband-to-be in what circumstances?

_____ **A.** Decoding anti-British secrets in the Great War

_____ **B.** Awaiting trial for the murder of her lover

_____ **C.** Working at Piccadilly Circus as a sword swallower

_____ **D.** At Cambridge, where they both were students

7. Georgia Cavendish marries Nigel Strangeways but does not abandon her career. What is her profession?

_____ **A.** Social worker

_____ **B.** Explorer

_____ **C.** Professional golfer

_____ **D.** Governess

8. Following the death of his wife, Georgia, Nigel Strangeways develops a relationship with which one of the following women?

_____ **A.** Clare Massenger, a sculptor

_____ **B.** Janet Guthrie, a race car driver

_____ **C.** Madge Critten, an actress

_____ **D.** Madeline Cranmere, an heiress

9. Who spent her wedding night in an isolated house with a corpse in the cellar?

_____ **A.** Harriet Vane

_____ **B.** Sonia Wayward

_____ **C.** Mrs. Danvers

_____ **D.** Honey West

10. Who tracks down her detective husband's killers?

_____ **A.** Nora Charles

_____ **B.** Arlette Van der Valk

_____ **C.** Tuppence Beresford

_____ **D.** Emmy Tibbett

11. In which way does Amanda Campion tell her husband, Albert, the identity of the murderer in *More Work for the Undertaker?*

_____ **A.** Underlining keywords in the *London Times*

_____ **B.** Over the telephone

_____ **C.** A cleverly concealed note in a Chinese fortune cookie

_____ **D.** A postscript in a letter

12. Emma Lathen's button-down widower detective, John Putnam Thatcher, could not manage his business and sleuthing affairs without the help of his secretary. Name her.

_____ **A.** Ms. Corsaut

_____ **B.** Miss Corset

_____ **C.** Mrs. Corbet

_____ **D.** Miss Corsa

13. Handsome, urbane Scotland Yard detective Alleyn Grant has a lady friend who is employed as which of the following?

_____ **A.** Actress

_____ **B.** Stewardess

_____ **C.** Teacher

_____ **D.** Zoo keeper

14. Velda is the attractive secretary-assistant to which bachelor detective?

_____ **A.** Mike Hammer

_____ **B.** Philip Marlowe

_____ **C.** Alfred Hitchcock

_____ **D.** Ellery Queen

15. Professor Kate Fansler, academic supersleuth, is married to which of the following?

_____ **A.** A chef

_____ **B.** A coroner

_____ **C.** A deputy district attorney

_____ **D.** A mystery writer

JUST FRIENDS?

Single, married, divorced, widowed—which marital status applies to the following detectives? Mark S, M, D, or W, and score 3 points for each correct answer.

1. Inspector French   _____
2. Inspector Harry Martineau   _____
3. Lew Archer   _____
4. Adam Dalgliesh   _____
5. Hercule Poirot   _____
6. Nero Wolfe   _____
7. Maud Silver   _____
8. Chief Inspector Wexford   _____
9. Elaine Wagstaff   _____
10. Mike Hammer   _____

COUPLES AND THEIR ORIGINS

Match the detecting couples in the first column with their creators in the second column and score 5 points for each. Then match the detecting couple with one of their mysteries in the third column. Score 5 points for each.

1. Pat and Jean Abbott

2. Emily and Henry Bryce

3. Tommy and Tuppence Beresford

4. Mr. and Mrs. North

5. Nigel and Georgia Strangeways

A. Frances and Richard Lockridge

B. Margaret Scherf

C. Nicholas Blake

D. Frances Crane

E. Agatha Christie

i. *The Smiler with the Knife*

ii. *Thirteen White Tulips*

iii. *N or M*

iv. *The Diplomat and the Gold Piano*

v. *Murder by the Book*

SCORING

"Watson, stand next to the guy with the pipe...."	_____
Unlikely Partnerships	_____
Working with Them or Against Them	_____
His and Hers	_____
The Better Half	_____
Just Friends?	_____
Couples and Their Origins	_____
Chapter Total Score	_____

More Than Just Friends and Much More Than Just Friends — The Verdict

If you scored between 245 and 163	You could have Nick and Nora Charles over for dinner and have a lot to talk about.
If you scored between 162 and 81	You're short on friends, but Lew Archer might still pay you an occasional call.
If you scored between 80 and 0	Either you're a hardened criminal or you've just forgotten who your friends are.

WHERE?

*Murder witnessed from the soft cushions of
an evening train, murder lying quiet behind a
glass of port and cigar, murder under the
eiderdown; in such circumstances... all of us
can cope with crime.*

— ANONYMOUS

Location plays such a prominent role in detective fiction
that we have set aside a whole chapter to test your
knowledge on this subject. "Where" includes identifying
the towns and cities where well-known sleuths have
worked and crimes have occurred. We have also added
questions about the specific and unique environments in
which mysteries have unfolded.

Writers have caused us to shiver in manor houses
and on ships, in theaters and in train stations. In pursuit
of whodunit we have walked the corridors of down-and-
out hotels with hard-boiled private eyes, and accom-
panied more-elegant sleuths through the halls of the rich
and the mighty.

Crime takes us to bazaars, through sculleries,
forests, and back alleys; down ski slopes, to universities,
circuses, courtrooms, and hostelries. The following
questions will show how good a tourist you have been.

TRAVELERS OR HOMEBODIES

Some detectives take us around the world, or at least around their own country. Others bring the world to their own real or fictional locale. Which of the following wander, and which stay close to home?

Whether the detective usually has the opportunity, if not the inclination, to sleep in his or her own bed is the criterion for this quiz. Mark T for Traveler or H for Homebody. Score 3 points for each correct answer.

_____ 1. Inspector Van der Valk

_____ 2. Rabbi David Small

_____ 3. Inspector Purbright

_____ 4. Roderick Alleyn

_____ 5. Maud Silver

_____ 6. Asey Mayo

_____ 7. Archie Goodwin

_____ 8. Lew Archer

_____ 9. Sir Henry Merrivale

_____ 10. Chief Inspector Wexford

_____ 11. Mrs. Pollifax

_____ 12. Montague Egg

_____ 13. Philo Vance

_____ 14. Nero Wolfe

_____ 15. The Beresfords

THE DETECTIVE AT HOME

Some authors humanize their heroes by allowing us to enter their private abodes. The detective is at home and is receiving guests, you might say.

Number 221-B Baker Street is almost as well known as its famous tenant. Visiting Sherlock at home helps us learn more about him. We discover that Sherlock keeps his pipe tobacco in a Persian slipper, and that his unanswered correspondence is impaled on a jackknife on the mantelpiece. For all this, Sherlock is more human and approachable, and we look forward to return visits.

Score 3 points for each detective you can identify from the following descriptions.

1. This sleuth shares a West 87th Street Manhattan apartment with a man who often assists him on cases.

   _____ **A.** Lew Archer

   _____ **B.** Captain Duncan Maclain

   _____ **C.** Richard Queen

   _____ **D.** Philip Marlowe

2. During his bachelor days, this bland-faced, sometimes foolish-looking young man had digs above a London police station.

   _____ **A.** Anthony Eden

   _____ **B.** Bulldog Drummond

   _____ **C.** Bertram Lynch

   _____ **D.** Albert Campion

3. Upon retirement, this famous Chief Commissioner of Metropolitan Police settled on a country estate known as Long Dream. He wants to lead the life of a country gentleman, but crime continually interrupts his tranquillity.

_____ **A.** John Appleby

_____ **B.** The Baron

_____ **C.** Max Winter

_____ **D.** John Mannering

4. Never call the resident of this brownstone before 11:00 A.M. If you want the attention of this eccentric private investigator, your chances are improved if you wait until he has devoured a carefully prepared lunch. Better still, leave a message with his assistant, who will repeat it to him verbatim.

_____ **A.** Sheridan Haynes

_____ **B.** Nero Wolfe

_____ **C.** Simon Templar

_____ **D.** Harold Stassen

5. Talboys is the sixteenth-century house occupied by an elegant and aristocratic sleuth and his bride. The house is in the neighborhood where his bride spent her childhood.

_____ **A.** John Churchill

_____ **B.** Inspector Rudd

_____ **C.** Stanislaus Oates

_____ **D.** Lord Peter Wimsey

6. His home is a boat on the Fort Lauderdale water-front. He won the boat in a poker game and named it *The Busted Flush.* Who is he?

_____ **A.** Travis McGee

_____ **B.** Bat Masterson

_____ **C.** Mike Hammer

_____ **D.** Kenny Rogers

7. Whose base of operations is *not* San Francisco?

_____ **A.** The Continental Op.

_____ **B.** Boston Blackie

_____ **C.** Lew Archer

_____ **D.** Sam Spade

8. The location is East Anglia at Fenchurch St. Paul. Lord Peter displays an arcane knowledge of church-bell ringing. Name the novel.

_____ **A.** *Murder at the Vicarage*

_____ **B.** *Nine Tailors*

_____ **C.** *Whose Body*

_____ **D.** *Death Under Sail*

9. Agatha Christie's *Cat Among the Pigeons* and Jose-phine Tey's *Miss Pym Disposes* have a similar setting. Name it.

_____ **A.** Girl's school

_____ **B.** Pet shop

_____ **C.** Newsroom

_____ **D.** Castle tower

10. Jane Marple is a shrewd judge of character. She says that she has learned all about human nature by observing life in her own village of:

_____ **A.** Meade St. Mary

_____ **B.** St. Mark's Meadow

_____ **C.** St. Mary's Meade

_____ **D.** Markington's Meade

11. Which setting is a favorite of detective writer Dick Francis?

_____ **A.** Circuses

_____ **B.** Theaters

_____ **C.** Racetracks

_____ **D.** New York City

12. Sleuths have been uncovering injustice for centuries. Judge Dee is a seventh-century magistrate who tracks criminals in which place?

_____ **A.** India

_____ **B.** Tahiti

_____ **C.** China

_____ **D.** Timbuktu

WHERE THEY HANG THEIR HATS

With which geographical setting do you associate each of the following? Some are authors, others are sleuths and important characters. Score 3 points for each correct answer.

1. Asey Mayo

    _____ **A.** Scottish Highlands

    _____ **B.** French Riviera

    _____ **C.** Cape Cod

    _____ **D.** Florida Keys

2. Nicholas Freeling

    _____ **A.** New Amsterdam

    _____ **B.** Holland

    _____ **C.** Moscow

    _____ **D.** Liechtenstein

3. Lew Archer

    _____ **A.** Bermuda

    _____ **B.** Kenosha

    _____ **C.** Miami

    _____ **D.** Los Angeles

4. Martin Beck

    _____ **A.** Stockholm

    _____ **B.** Salonika

    _____ **C.** Sandwich Islands

    _____ **D.** Sardinia

5. Mabel Seeley

    _____ **A.** Minnesota

    _____ **B.** Alaska

_____ **C.** Peking

_____ **D.** Arkansas

6. Leslie Ford

   _____ **A.** Detroit

   _____ **B.** Rio de Janeiro

   _____ **C.** Washington, D.C.

   _____ **D.** Plattsburgh

7. Ngaio Marsh

   _____ **A.** Louisiana

   _____ **B.** New Zealand

   _____ **C.** Bombay

   _____ **D.** Manhattan

8. Ursula Curtiss

   _____ **A.** New York

   _____ **B.** Juneau, Alaska

   _____ **C.** Oslo, Norway

   _____ **D.** Albuquerque, New Mexico

9. Maurice Procter

   _____ **A.** Egypt

   _____ **B.** England

   _____ **C.** Ecuador

   _____ **D.** Ethiopia

10. Robert Van Gulik

_____ **A.** Capetown, South Africa

_____ **B.** Botswana

_____ **C.** China

_____ **D.** Darien, Connecticut

HOMETOWNS

Score 3 points for each correct answer.

_____   **1.** What sleuth goes to work at the Quai des Orfevres?

_____   **2.** Who lives on West 35th Street?

_____   **3.** Which Inspector is associated with Centre Street?

_____   **4.** Which sleuth solves crimes in Flaxborough?

_____   **5.** Who works at Hollywood's Wilcox Avenue police station?

_____   **6.** Who lives in a New York East 60s residence with his wife, son, and cat?

_____   **7.** The 87th Precinct, located on the mythical island of Isola, is home to which detective?

_____   **8.** Which cop works at the Honolulu Police Department?

_____ **9.** What supersleuth, famous for the adage "Crime does not pay," pursues gangsters in a city that resembles Chicago?

_____ **10.** Which Los Angeles–based sleuth loves foreign cars and is independently wealthy?

A. Henry Gamadge

B. Inspector Purbright

C. Dick Tracy

D. Maigret

E. Inspector McKee

F. Sergeant Luis Mendoza

G. Nero Wolfe

H. Steve Carella

I. Charlie Chan

J. Ivor Maddox

FOUL PLAY

A number of detective fiction novels use sports as part of the plot and setting. Fill in the correct sport for each book title. Score 6 points for each correct answer.

1. _The Bishop Murder Case_ by S.S. Van Dine

_____

2. _Death and the Leaping Ladies_ by Charles Drummond

_____

3. _Forfeit_ by Dick Francis

_____

4. *The Name of the Game Is Murder* by Eliot Asinof

  _____

5. *The Crack in the Tea Cup* by Michael Gilbert

  _____

6. *An Awkward Lie* by Michael Innes

  _____

7. *Saturday Games* by Brown Meggs

  _____

8. *Silent Witness* by Margaret Yorke

  _____

9. *Alibi Innings* by Barbara Worsley Gough

  _____

10. *The Devil to Play* by Leonard Holton

  _____

11. *The Problem of the Wire Cage* by John Dickson Carr

  _____

12. *Fer de Lance* by Rex Stout

  _____

13. *The Screwball King Murder* by Kin Platt

  _____

SCORING

Travelers or Homebodies	_____
The Detective at Home	_____
Where They Hang Their Hats	_____
Hometowns	_____
Foul Play	_____
Chapter Total Score	_____

The Verdict

If you scored between 219 and 146
You know where all the bodies are buried.

If you scored between 145 and 73
You've got a few skeletons in your closet.

If you scored between 72 and 0
You might as well check under the chair you're sitting on—you've missed everywhere else.

WHODUNIT AND

WHY?

It is one of the hectic pleasures of reading about crime that we can switch sides constantly. We can commit murder in the morning, and catch ourselves in the afternoon.

> —TIMES LITERARY SUPPLEMENT
> February 1955

The *who* in "whodunit" is the one essential ingredient in all crime fiction. Sad to say, our detective heroes cannot exist unless someone commits a crime—preferably murder.

Even if the victim is the most despicable sort, the crime must be solved. Our hero must unravel the mystery of whodunit for the good of society—or at least the peace of mind of the reader.

Discovering whodunit keeps the professional detective employed, the amateur sleuth occupied, and the rest of us involved in the chase.

In order to avoid revealing whodunit in stories you have yet to read, we have limited the following questions to those criminals whose identities are well known. We have tried to be fair, but since we are dealing with rascals and villains, expect the very worst.

FALLEN ARCHES

Choose the right archfiend in the following questions. Score 3 points for each correct answer.

1. What brilliant and thoroughly evil villain of numerous stories was known as the "devil doctor"?

   _____ **A.** Dr. Faust

   _____ **B.** Dr. Gideon Fell

   _____ **C.** Dr. Jekyll

   _____ **D.** Dr. Fu Manchu

2. Which archvillain was known to many as a mild-mannered professor of mathematics?

   _____ **A.** Dr. Teddy Bickleigh

   _____ **B.** James Moriarty

   _____ **C.** Lothrop Mittenthal

   _____ **D.** Sidney Greenstreet

3. Who was Bulldog Drummond's major adversary (aside from Germans and Russians)?

   _____ **A.** John Wilson

   _____ **B.** Uriah Heep

   _____ **C.** Henry Nash

   _____ **D.** Carl Peterson

4. Father Brown's greatest triumph is tracking, catching, and reforming which nefarious criminal?

_____ **A.** Flambeau

_____ **B.** Mycroft

_____ **C.** Julie Killeen

_____ **D.** The Spider

5. Name the group of criminals who try to force Michael Lanyard (The Lone Wolf) to join them in their evil deeds.

_____ **A.** The Flock

_____ **B.** KAOS

_____ **C.** SMERSH

_____ **D.** The Pack

6. Which notorious jewel thief posed by day as John Mannering, a respectable antique dealer?

_____ **A.** The Duke

_____ **B.** The Baron

_____ **C.** The Cat

_____ **D.** The Scavenger

7. Thief Romney Pringle also had a legitimate occupation. What was this more honest job?

_____ **A.** Literary agent

_____ **B.** Prison warden

_____ **C.** Bank president

_____ **D.** Potato chip manufacturer

8. Which of the following fictional bad guys wrote mystery novels?

_____ **A.** Ganesh Ghote

_____ **B.** Gordon Craigie

_____ **C.** Caroline Keene

_____ **D.** Anthony Trent

9. Which of the following, created by Sax Rohmer, is a female Fu Manchu with as many evil tricks up her sleeve?

_____ **A.** Suburu

_____ **B.** Sweet Sue Manchu

_____ **C.** Sumuru

_____ **D.** Su Nee

10. Which of the following fictional villains was dealt with by Dick Tracy?

_____ **A.** Gabby

_____ **B.** Flattop

_____ **C.** The Gopher

_____ **D.** Fat Face

EYEWITNESS ACCOUNTS

From the eyewitness descriptions, identify the crook in the lineup and score 4 points for each correct answer.

1. *Vital statistics:* Short, stumpy body; pale blue eyes; fiery red hair.
   Charge: He was hired by SMERSH to steal the gold from Fort Knox.
   Lineup:

   _____ **A.** Auric Goldfinger

   _____ **B.** Hugo Drax

   _____ **C.** George Zucco

   _____ **D.** Johnny Paycheck

2. *Vital statistics:* Athletic build; blue eyes; remarkably handsome; known as an outstanding cricket player.
   Charge: He is a master safecracker.
   Lineup:

   _____ **A.** Wilfred Dover

   _____ **B.** Dudley Diggs

   _____ **C.** Raffles

   _____ **D.** The Infallible Goodahl

3. *Vital statistics:* Tall; broad-shouldered; thinning and graying hair; beady-eyed.
   Charge: He is an attorney who twists and manipulates the law for his own advancement and his clients' gain.[1]

FOOTPRINT

[1] Many lawyers claim that this is not a punishable offense.

Lineup:

_____ **A.** Robert Reed

_____ **B.** Caspar Gutman

_____ **C.** Nick Velvet

_____ **D.** Randolph Mason

4. *Vital statistics:* Tall; thin; aristocratic-looking; has the ability to change his appearance quite dramatically without the use of makeup; ruthless.
Charge: He has been a thief since childhood.
Lineup:

_____ **A.** The Whistler

_____ **B.** Hamilton Cleek

_____ **C.** William Sonder

_____ **D.** Lon Chaney

WHYDUNITS

Indicate whether the following motives for murderous behavior are True or False. In all cases, the names and actions are true and only the motives may have been changed ... Score 4 points for each correct answer.

1. In Ellery Queen's *Cat of Many Tails,* the doctor's wife killed many people because she was a drug addict. True or False?

2. In *The Documents in the Case* by Dorothy Sayers and Robert Eustace, Harwood Lathom murdered the husband of the beautiful Margaret Harrison. Lathom hoped to marry Margaret.   True or False?

3. Twelve travelers in *Murder on the Orient Express* by Agatha Christie stabbed Mr. Ratchett to death because they were greedy heirs to his fortune. True or False?

4. In *Farewell, My Lovely* by Raymond Chandler, Velma, the former girlfriend of an ex-convict and currently the wife of a politically powerful man, is responsible for various and assorted murders done for revenge. True or False?

5. In Ross MacDonald's *The Goodbye Look*, Larry Chalmers kills several people in order to protect them from evil. True or False?

6. A model is murdered in Vera Caspary's book *Laura* because of mistaken identity. True or False?

7. In *Died in the Wool* by Ngaio Marsh, Florence (Flossie) Rubrick is murdered by her nephew, Douglas Grace, and packed in a bale of wool. He killed her because he thought she was a spy. True or False?

8. In *The Spiral Staircase* by Ethel Lina White, a mute girl is threatened by a murderer who has a maniacal urge to rid the world of imperfection. True or False?

9. In *Nerve* by Dick Francis, a jockey is driven to commit suicide. The sinister "hands on the reins" belong to an asthmatic sportscaster whose own career in racing was frustrated by his illness. True or False?

10. In *The Maltese Falcon* by Dashiell Hammett, Brigid O'Shaughnessy kills Sam Spade's partner, Miles Archer, because he was against home rule for Ireland. True or False?

CLASSIC CASES

Score 5 points for each correct answer.

1. From the clues in the word game below, identify the correct mystery novel.

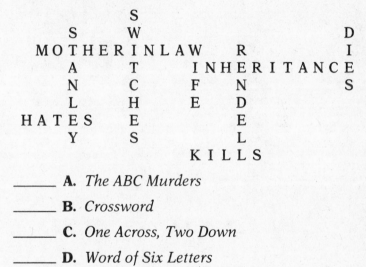

```
                S
     S          W                            D
   M O T H E R I N L A W     R               I
     A          T       I N H E R I T A N C E
     N          C       F     N             S
     L          H       E     D
   H A T E S    E             E
     Y          S             L
                        K I L L S
```

_____ **A.** *The ABC Murders*

_____ **B.** *Crossword*

_____ **C.** *One Across, Two Down*

_____ **D.** *Word of Six Letters*

2. Which classic mystery novel is summarized in the following newspaper headlines?

SECRETARY FOUND MURDERED

UNIDENTIFIED BODY FOUND
IN LABORATORY BASEMENT

PROMINENT INVENTOR MISSING
PRIME SUSPECT DISAPPEARS

DOG BREAKS CASE!

_____ **A.** *The Hound of the Baskervilles* by Arthur Conan Doyle

_____ **B.** *The Thin Man* by Dashiell Hammett

_____ **C.** *Mortal Remains* by Margaret Yorke

_____ **D.** *Dog's Ransom* by Patricia Highsmith

3. From the newspaper headlines below, choose the correct Raymond Chandler mystery novel.

GENERAL'S YOUNGEST DAUGHTER BLACKMAILED

BLACKMAILER FOUND DEAD
IN LAUREL CANYON "LOVE NEST"

PHILIP MARLOWE SOLVES FIRST CASE

_____ **A.** *The Little Sister*

_____ **B.** *The Big Sleep*

_____ **C.** *The Long Goodbye*

_____ **D.** *Double Indemnity*

4. From the newspaper headlines choose the correct mystery novel.

NIGHTGOWN-CLAD WOMAN FOUND
MURDERED IN CLERGYMAN'S CAR

CHIEF OF POLICE AND DAVID SMALL
TEAM UP TO SOLVE MYSTERY

POLICE OFFICER FOUND GUILTY
FEARED BLACKMAIL

_____ **A.** *The Poetical Policeman* by Edgar Wallace

_____ **B.** *The Case of the Stuttering Bishop* by Erle Stanley Gardner

_____ **C.** *The Wisdom of Father Brown* by G. K. Chesterton

_____ **D.** *Friday the Rabbi Slept Late* by Harry Kemelman

5. In what mystery novel does a wealthy woman retain Nero Wolfe to find out why the FBI is having her followed?

_____ **A.** *The Walking Shadow*

_____ **B.** *The Man in the Moonlight*

_____ **C.** *In the Best Families*

_____ **D.** *The Doorbell Rang*

6. When a wealthy elderly woman is found murdered, the young man who was recently named her heir is the prime suspect. During the trial his wife gives damaging evidence against him, but she is discredited by the clever defense attorney. A surprise ending makes this short story a detective fiction classic. Name it.

_____ **A.** *Question of Proof* by Nicholas Blake

_____ **B.** *Witness for the Prosecution* by Agatha Christie

_____ **C.** *In the Teeth of the Evidence* by Dorothy L. Sayers

_____ **D.** *Where There's a Will* by Rex Stout

7. Ten people are invited by an unknown host to be houseguests on an isolated island. A recording device reveals the past crime committed by each of the guests. One guest after another is murdered un-

til all are dead, including a retired judge — the self-appointed avenger. What is the book?

_____ **A.** *Flowers for the Judge* by Margery Allingham

_____ **B.** *The Verdict of Twelve* by Raymond Postgate

_____ **C.** *Ten Little Indians* by Agatha Christie

_____ **D.** *I, the Jury* by Mickey Spillane

8. In this "locked room" mystery, a Christmas party turns from unpleasant to foul when the acid-tongued host is murdered. The victim's nephew becomes the prime suspect when Inspector Hemingway discovers he is the principal heir. A missing book provides Hemingway with the vital clue. The "sweetness and light" brother of the victim proves to be the guilty party. Name the book.

_____ **A.** *Envious Casca* by Georgette Heyer

_____ **B.** *The Traveler Returns* by Patricia Wentworth

_____ **C.** *The Blue Room* by Georges Simenon

_____ **D.** *Call for the Dead* by John le Carré

9. Dolores Gonzales does not kill for money but for love. The lover she cannot bear to lose is Steelgrave. When a former associate of Steelgrave's turns up with blackmail on his mind, Dolores and an accomplice murder him. She then kills the accomplice, as she is fearful that his mental instability will lead to his revealing the truth. Steelgrave becomes victim number three when Dolores discovers he is unfaithful to her. Our detective hero knows all, but he has no proof. Dolores is finally brought to justice by her former husband, who kills her as punishment for ruining his life. In what book does this happen?

_____ **A.** *Sudden Vengeance* by Edmond Crispin

_____ **B.** *The Little Sister* by Raymond Chandler

_____ **C.** *The Evil Friendship* by Vin Racker

_____ **D.** *The Man Who Lost His Wife* by Julian Symons

10. The disappearance of Robert, a prominent San Diego rancher, rekindles interest in a double murder that took place ten years earlier. Robert's psychotically overprotective mother had done away with both her husband and Robert's lover to "protect" her son. We discover that Robert was murdered by the son of his ranch foreman, but it is the psychological twists that uncover his mother's crimes which give this plot its unique flavor. What is the book?

_____ **A.** *Unexpected Night* by Elizabeth Daly

_____ **B.** *Beyond This Point Are Monsters* by Margaret Millar

_____ **C.** *They Buried a Man* by Mildred Davis

_____ **D.** *Night of the Twelfth* by Michael Gilbert

11. Hard-boiled good guy Mike Hammer vows vengeance against the killer of the man who saved his life in World War II. After chapters of hot pursuit, Hammer corners and kills the murderer, whose dying words are "How could you?" Hammer's "It was easy" is one of our favorite literary responses. Which of these Mickey Spillane novels tells this tale?

_____ **A.** *Vengeance Is Mine*

_____ **B.** *Day of the Guns*

_____ **C.** *Survival Zero*

_____ **D.** *I, the Jury*

12. In which mystery novel is police commissioner That-cher Colt scheduled for death by a mad scientist who has discovered an untraceable method of murder?

_____ **A.** *Nightmare in Dublin* by Philip Loraine

_____ **B.** *The Shudders* by Anthony Abbot

_____ **C.** *Case Is Closed* by Pat Wentworth

_____ **D.** *Killing Time* by Donald Westlake

13. The captain of a yacht cruising off the coast of Eng-land is found shot. The passengers come ashore and are housed in a cottage, in which the police inquiries are conducted. Through the insights of an unassum-ing civil servant on vacation who assists the more self-assured Detective Sergeant Birrell, the mystery of whodunit is solved. What is the title of this nauti-cal mystery?

_____ **A.** *The Sea Mystery* by Freeman Wills Croft

_____ **B.** *Brighton Rock* by Graham Greene

_____ **C.** *For Kicks* by Dick Francis

_____ **D.** *Death Under Sail* by C. P. Snow

14. An ex-courtesan turned poet is the most obvious suspect in this triple-murder case. Although our de-tective knows the suspect is innocent, he has no evi-dence with which to convict the sadistic killer. At a festival, our detective-magistrate lays out his case against the murderer. When the poet senses that our detective is closing in on the killer, she confesses to the crimes, motivated by her long-standing love for the killer. The murderer's pride will not allow a former whore to save him, and he commits suicide in full view of the horrified guests. What is the title?

_____ **A.** *Poets and Murder*

_____ **B.** *Moto's Dissertation*

_____ **C.** *The Emperor's Pearl*

_____ **D.** *Charlie Chan in Poo-Yang*

15. When solo violinist Lucy Carless is strangled during the intermission of a Markshire Orchestra concert, suspects abound. Possible murderers include her first husband and his second wife; her jealous new husband; a womanizer who plays the organ in the Markshire Orchestra; a clarinetist and fellow Polish countryman with whom she'd had a violent argument — to name a few. A reference to Charles Dickens and an arcane bit of English law regarding peerage are two key clues. A knowledge of Mozart can help the reader solve this cleverly plotted whodunit. Name the book.

_____ **A.** *When the Wind Blows* by Cyril Hare

_____ **B.** *The Air That Kills* by Margaret Millar

_____ **C.** *Death Takes a Bow* by Frances and Richard Lockridge

_____ **D.** *The Death of an Artist* by John Rhode

ETERNAL NEMESES

Match the detectives on the left with their villainous adversaries on the right. Score 5 points for each correct answer.

_____ **1.** Inspector Martineau   **A.** Arnold Zeck

_____ **2.** The Fugitive   **B.** Fidelity Dove

_____ **3.** Gabriel Syme   **C.** Dr. Fu Manchu

_____ **4.** Nero Wolfe   **D.** Supreme Council of Seven

_____ **5.** Sir Denis Nayland Smith   **E.** Dixie Costello

_____ **6.** Detective Inspector Rason   **F.** The One-Armed Man

SCORING

Fallen Arches   _____

Eyewitness Accounts   _____

Whydunits   _____

Classic Cases   _____

Eternal Nemeses   _____

      Chapter Total Score   _____

The Verdict

**If you scored
between 191 and 127**

You are an excellent judge of character.

**If you scored
between 126 and 63**

You know your crooks, but the subtleties of the criminal mind evade you.

**If you scored
between 62 and 0**

You're a likely victim.

DICKS

OF THE

FLICKS

*Just as a devotee of cricket will spend happy
winter evenings compiling imaginary teams
of the greatest ever, so will the detective addict set himself up as a one-man collection
committee to choose the classics of his kind.*

—C. DAY LEWIS

In the beginning, there was the Saturday afternoon
matinee. There we met Charlie Chan, Philip Marlowe,
Sam Spade, Mr. Moto, the Saint, and scores more who
were to become lifelong friends.

Later, the matinees gave way to original novels,
although the cycle repeated itself years later, when we
met the dashing Mr. Bond on the screen and went from
there to Ian Fleming's books.

Always there was Hitchcock, the great master, who
so often showed us the work of great mystery writers on
the screen and sent us into the bookstore for more.

Whether what we see on the screen is less valid as an
experience of the imagination than what we read on the
page is up to other people to decide—we'll take our detectives any way we can get them. Getting them in a dark
theater with a couple of hundred other mystery lovers is
fine with us.

CRIME ON THE SILVER SCREEN

Score 3 points for each correct answer.

1. The third actor to play the Falcon was John Calvert. Tim Conway was the second, and his brother preceded him. Who was the first movie Falcon?

   _____ **A.** Ralph Richardson

   _____ **B.** George Sanders

   _____ **C.** Charles Bronson

   _____ **D.** Lionel Barrymore

2. Ronald Colman and David Niven both played the charming Raffles in American films. Choose the actor who first introduced this roguish character to American audiences in a feature-length film.

   _____ **A.** Gene Kelly

   _____ **B.** C. Aubrey Smith

   _____ **C.** John Barrymore

   _____ **D.** Leon Ames

3. Which of the following actors has played the immortal Sherlock Holmes in films?

   _____ **A.** John Barrymore

   _____ **B.** Raymond Massey

   _____ **C.** Robert Stephens

   _____ **D.** Basil Rathbone

   _____ **E.** Clive Brook

_____ **F.** Peter Cushing

_____ **G.** All of the above

4. Raymond Chandler's Philip Marlowe has been played by all but one of the following actors. Who did not play Marlowe?

_____ **A.** Dick Powell

_____ **B.** George Montgomery

_____ **C.** Robert Montgomery

_____ **D.** Humphrey Bogart

_____ **E.** Glenn Ford

_____ **F.** James Garner

_____ **G.** Robert Mitchum

5. Mr. Moto, John P. Marquand's canny detective, was played by which actor?

_____ **A.** Keye Luke

_____ **B.** Peter Lorre

_____ **C.** Charlie Chan

_____ **D.** Anthony Quinn

6. William Powell was known to filmgoers as two of these famous dicks. Which two? (Score 6 points if you get them both right.)

_____ **A.** Philo Vance

_____ **B.** Arsène Lupin

_____ **C.** Nick Charles

_____ **D.** Lew Archer

_____ **E.** Ellery Queen

_____ **F.** Nero Wolfe

7. In the film version of Eric Ambler's *The Mask Of Dimitrios,* Peter Lorre played which character?

  _____ **A.** A Polish priest

  _____ **B.** A Spanish dancer

  _____ **C.** A Finnish forger

  _____ **D.** A Dutch novelist

  _____ **E.** All of the above

8. There have been three film versions of Agatha Christie's *Ten Little Indians.* In the 1944 version, who played the murderer?

  _____ **A.** Roland Young

  _____ **B.** Arthur Godfrey

  _____ **C.** Barry Fitzgerald

  _____ **D.** Alec Guinness

9. Ross Macdonald's Lew Archer was played in two films by which actor?

  _____ **A.** Paul Newman

  _____ **B.** Steve McQueen

  _____ **C.** Robert Redford

  _____ **D.** Edward G. Robinson

10. What mystery sleuth did Sidney Toler, Warner Oland, J. Carroll Nash, and Roland Winter play?

  _____ **A.** Sam Spade

  _____ **B.** Charlie Chan

  _____ **C.** The Shadow

  _____ **D.** Fu Manchu

11. The Alfred Hitchcock film of Daphne du Maurier's *Rebecca* costarred which actress as the sinister housekeeper?

_____ **A.** Miriam Hopkins

_____ **B.** Gale Sondergaard

_____ **C.** Florence Henderson

_____ **D.** Judith Anderson

12. *Strangers on a Train* by Patricia Highsmith, *Double Indemnity* by James M. Cain, and *The Unseen* by Ethel Lina White were adapted for the screen. Which mystery writer was a coauthor of all three screenplays?

_____ **A.** Patricia Moyes

_____ **B.** Raymond Chandler

_____ **C.** Ellery Queen

_____ **D.** Dashiell Hammett

13. Charlotte Armstrong's novel *Mischief* was presented on the screen as *Don't Bother to Knock*. Who costarred in the film as the baby-sitter?

_____ **A.** Mary Beth Hughes

_____ **B.** Deanna Durbin

_____ **C.** Marilyn Monroe

_____ **D.** Jane Withers

14. A radio mystery narrator, played by Claude Rains, makes a public confession of murder in a film bear-

ing the same name as one of the following books.
Choose the correct book.

_____ **A.** *The Long Goodbye* by Raymond Chandler

_____ **B.** *Dirty Story* by Eric Ambler

_____ **C.** *The Radio Detective* by Arthur B. Reeve

_____ **D.** *The Unsuspected* by Charlotte Armstrong

15. The films *The Spiral Staircase* and *The Lady Vanishes* were based on books by which author?

_____ **A.** Mabel Seeley

_____ **B.** Phoebe Atwood Taylor

_____ **C.** Vera Caspary

_____ **D.** Ethel Lina White

16. Which of the following films were made from books by Donald B. Westlake? (Score 3 points for each correct answer and subtract 2 points for each bad guess.)

_____ **A.** *The Hot Rock*

_____ **B.** *Cops and Robbers*

_____ **C.** *Hopscotch*

_____ **D.** *Bank Shot*

17. Captain Duncan Maclain is a New York detective with a fondness for books, music, and his seeing-eye dog. Which actor played this blind man in two films made in the 1940s?

_____ **A.** Van Johnson

_____ **B.** Roland Young

_____ **C.** Robert Young

_____ **D.** Edward Arnold

18. Identify the actresses closely associated with film detectives Sam Spade and Nick Charles. (Score 3 points for each correct answer and subtract 2 points for each wrong one.)

_____ **A.** Myrna Loy

_____ **B.** Shirley Temple

_____ **C.** Lauren Bacall

_____ **D.** Mary Astor

_____ **E.** Priscilla Lane

_____ **F.** Wanda Hendrix

_____ **G.** Lucille Ball

19. The mystery film *The Lady of Burlesque,* starring Barbara Stanwyck, was originally a whodunit entitled *The G-String Murders.* Who wrote it?

_____ **A.** Pat Wentworth

_____ **B.** Leslie Ford

_____ **C.** Mildred Davis

_____ **D.** Gyspy Rose Lee

20. In which films does Miss Marple appear? (Score 3 points for each correct answer; subtract 2 points for each wrong answer.)

_____ **A.** *Murder at the Gallop*

_____ **B.** *Murder Most Foul*

_____ **C.** *Murder by Death*

_____ **D.** *Murder at the Cinema*

_____ **E.** *Murder Takes a Bow*

_____ **F.** *Murder Ahoy*

CHANDLER ON FILM

Match the Raymond Chandler mystery novels on the left with the film versions on the right. Score 3 points for each correct answer. (Some novels have been filmed more than once.)

_____	**1.** *Farewell, My Lovely*	**A.** *Time to Kill*
_____	**2.** *The High Window*	**B.** *The Falcon Takes Over*
_____	**3.** *The Little Sister*	**C.** *Marlowe*
		D. *Murder My Sweet*
		E. *The Brasher Doubloon*

THE BARRYMORE GANG

Which Barrymore appeared in which film? Mark E for Ethel, J for John, and L for Lionel. Score 3 points for each correct identification. (One film stars more than one Barrymore, so score 6 points if you correctly identify both Barrymores.)

1. *The Spiral Staircase* _____

2. *Arsène Lupin* _____

3. *Bulldog Drummond Comes Back* _____

4. *Moss Rose* _____

5. *Moonrise* _____

6. *Key Largo* _____

7. *Night Club Scandal* _____

8. *The Devil Doll* _____

9. *The Paradine Case* _____

10. *Portrait of Jenny* _____

GRANT'S LEADING LADIES

Match the Cary Grant films on the left with his leading ladies on the right. Score 2 points for each correct answer.

_____ 1. *North by Northwest*   **A.** Ingrid Bergman

_____ 2. *Notorious*   **B.** Joan Fontaine

_____ 3. *To Catch a Thief*   **C.** Audrey Hepburn

_____ 4. *Suspicion*   **D.** Eva Marie Saint

_____ 5. *Charade*   **E.** Grace Kelly

ACTORS IN SERIES

Match the film series detectives on the left with the movie actors on the right. Score 3 points for each correct answer.

_____ 1. Michael Shayne   A. John Howard

_____ 2. Lone Wolf   B. Margaret Rutherford

_____ 3. Bulldog
Drummond   C. Peter Lorre

_____ 4. Boston Blackie   D. Warren William

_____ 5. Crime Doctor   E. Ralph Bellamy

_____ 6. Ellery Queen   F. Lloyd Nolan

_____ 7. Mr. Moto   G. Warner Baxter

_____ 8. Nancy Drew   H. Ralph Byrd

_____ 9. Miss Marple   I. Chester Morris

_____ 10. Dick Tracy   J. Bonita Granville

MODUS OPERANDI

Match the clues on the left with the movie titles on the right. Score 2 points for each correct answer.

_____	**1.** Poison pen	**A.**	*The 39 Steps*
_____	**2.** Harry Lime	**B.**	*Call Northside 777*
_____	**3.** Scotland	**C.**	*The 13th Letter*
_____	**4.** Christie	**D.**	*The 3rd Man*
_____	**5.** Reporter	**E.**	*The 7 Percent Solution*
_____	**6.** Freud	**F.**	*Ten Little Indians*

FEMME FATALES

Match the women on the left with the actresses on the right. Score 3 points for each correct answer.

_____	**1.** Woman in Green	**A.**	Ida Lupino
_____	**2.** Woman in the Window	**B.**	Hillary Brooke
_____	**3.** Woman in White	**C.**	Ann Sheridan
_____	**4.** Woman of Straw	**D.**	Joan Bennett
_____	**5.** Woman on the Run	**E.**	Eleanor Parker
_____	**6.** Woman in Hiding	**F.**	Gina Lollobrigida

DEATH AT 32 FRAMES PER SECOND

Choose the appropriate film from each of the following descriptions. Score 4 points for each correct answer.

1. Hypochondria turns Leona into an invalid. One night she accidentally overhears a phone conversation in which her murder is being planned. Leona's husband is desperate for the insurance money he will receive if his plot succeeds. She is unable to convince the police she is in danger because of her reputation as a crank caller. Consequently, Leona has to await the inevitable horror.

   _____ A. *The Woman Who Cried Wolf*

   _____ B. *The Telephone Only Rings Twice*

   _____ C. *No Way to Treat a Lady*

   _____ D. *Sorry, Wrong Number*

2. Uncle Charlie visits his relatives. His niece discovers the secrets of his past: Charlie murdered three wives for their money. If his niece reveals her knowledge of his crimes, she will almost certainly become his fourth victim. Fortunately, Charlie dies, and only his niece knows that his very respectable funeral is a sham.

   _____ A. *Shadow of a Doubt*

   _____ B. *Charlie's Niece*

   _____ C. *Boomerang*

   _____ D. *Dial M for Murder*

3. Because he can't shake off his past, a small-time criminal lands in jail on a twenty-year robbery sentence. He loyally refuses to inform on the others who are involved in the holdup, until he learns of the serious consequences of his conviction on his family. A vicious psychopath hounds him after he informs. He lures the psychopath out in the open through a clever ruse, but is seriously wounded in the effort. He recovers, and hopes—at the film's end—that he will be able to avoid crime in the future.

_____ **A.** *The Fatalist*

_____ **B.** *Trials of an Epicene*

_____ **C.** *Kiss of Death*

_____ **D.** *The Informer*

4. Death comes to a former pugilist who had allowed his career to be taken over by racketeers. A beautiful but deceitful woman lured the ex-boxer into double-crossing the gang. A diligent insurance investigator uncovers her treachery in this triple-cross mystery film.

_____ **A.** *Confession*

_____ **B.** *The Killers*

_____ **C.** *Madison Square Garden*

_____ **D.** *The Boxer and the Lady*

5. Fierce jealousy was the motive that drove the sophisticated Waldo Lydecker to commit murder—better to kill than to lose the beautiful woman he possessed. Unknowingly, he murders the wrong woman in his intended victim's apartment. The dead woman is so disfigured that even the police mistake the identity of the corpse. A dogged detective uncovers the murderer and wins the love of the supposed victim.

_____ **A.** *Laura*

_____ **B.** *Whatever Happened to Vivian Blaine*

_____ **C.** *Murder My Suite*

_____ **D.** *Deadly Encounter*

6. Johnnie Aysgarth is charming, unprincipled, and possibly a murderer. His shy wife believes that he plans to kill her for her money. Not true in this movie. (It *was* true in the Frances Iles book on which the film was based.)

_____ **A.** *Stella Dallas*

_____ **B.** *The Mirror*

_____ **C.** *Gaslight*

_____ **D.** *Suspicion*

7. An introverted professor is infatuated with a beautiful woman in a portrait. He becomes involved with a sensuous young woman who resembles her. Accidentally, the professor kills the young woman's jealous lover. He disposes of the body, but is then threatened with blackmail and the certainty of being pursued by the police. The professor decides to commit suicide by taking poison. Both the professor and the audience are relieved to discover the entire episode has been a nightmare.

_____ **A.** *Nightwatch*

_____ **B.** *Woman in the Window*

_____ **C.** *The Mona Lisa Affair*

_____ **D.** *Darkness Before Dawn*

8. A blind American playwright overhears a kidnap-
murder plot in a London pub, but can't convince the
police that he isn't suffering from an overactive
imagination. With the help of his butler and his
sweetheart, he solves the mystery, and in a climactic
last scene uses his handicap to advantage when he is
forced to kill his adversary.

_____ **A.** *Bats Fly Up*

_____ **B.** *Death on My Left*

_____ **C.** *23 Paces to Baker Street*

_____ **D.** *Dark Victory*

A TITLE SPELLED "B-O-X O-F-F-I-C-E"

For reasons best known to Hollywood, film titles often differ from the titles of the books on which they are based. Match the books on the left with their film version on the right. Score 4 points each.

1.	*The Amateur Cracksman* by Ernest William Hornung	A.	*The Saint's Vacation*
		B.	*Snowbound*
2.	*Family Skeleton* by Dorothy Miles Disney	C.	*The Innocents*
		D.	*Assignment Paris*
3.	*Before the Fact* by Francis Iles	E.	*Stella*
		F.	*Raffles*
4.	*Black Curtain* by Cornell Woolrich	G.	*Cape Fear*
5.	*Call for the Dead* by John le Carré	H.	*The Deadly Affair*
		I.	*Three's a Crowd*
6.	*The Executioners* by John D. MacDonald	J.	*The Street of Chance*
		K.	*House of Fear*
7.	*The Five Orange Pips* by Arthur Conan Doyle	L.	*Suspicion*
8.	*Getaway* by Leslie Charteris		
9.	*Hasty Wedding* by Mignon G. Eberhart		
10.	*The Lonely Skier* by Hammond Innes		
11.	*Trial by Terror* by Paul Gallico		
12.	*The Turn of the Screw* by Henry James		

LEADING MEN AND WOMEN

Below each of the following movie stars are films in which they may or may not have had a role. Score 3 points for identifying each film in each question in which the stars appeared.

1. Jimmy Stewart

    _____ **A.** *After the Thin Man*

    _____ **B.** *Rear Window*

    _____ **C.** *Vertigo*

    _____ **D.** *The Murder Man*

    _____ **E.** All of the above

2. Ray Milland

    _____ **A.** *Dial M for Murder*

    _____ **B.** *Charlie Chan in London*

    _____ **C.** *Bulldog Drummond Escapes*

    _____ **D.** *The Big Fix*

    _____ **E.** *The Champagne Murders*

3. Robert Montgomery

    _____ **A.** *The Lady in the Lake*

    _____ **B.** *Ride the Pink Horse*

    _____ **C.** *The Lady Vanishes*

    _____ **D.** *Murder, She Said*

    _____ **E.** *Night Must Fall*

4. Bette Davis

_____ **A.** *The Letter*

_____ **B.** *A Stolen Life*

_____ **C.** *Anatomy of an Epicene*

_____ **D.** *The Caper of the Golden Bulls*

_____ **E.** *Satan Met a Lady*

5. Fred MacMurray

_____ **A.** *Let's Kill Uncle*

_____ **B.** *Double Indemnity*

_____ **C.** *Murder, He Says*

_____ **D.** *Murder on the Orient Express*

_____ **E.** None of the above

6. Van Heflin

_____ **A.** *The Saint in Palm Springs*

_____ **B.** *Black Widow*

_____ **C.** *Murder Is My Business*

_____ **D.** *The Mistook Lorry*

_____ **E.** *The Man Who Knew Too Much*

7. Gloria Grahame

_____ **A.** *In a Lonely Place*

_____ **B.** *Dillinger*

_____ **C.** *Odd Man Out*

_____ **D.** *The Big Heat*

_____ **E.** *Shy Murderess*

8. Claire Trevor

_____ **A.** *The Murder Man*

_____ **B.** *Street of Chance*

_____ **C.** *Experiment Perilous*

_____ **D.** *The Lucky Stiff*

_____ **E.** *Murder My Sweet*

9. Richard Basehart

_____ **A.** *Ten Little Indians*

_____ **B.** *Cry Wolf*

_____ **C.** *House on Telegraph Hill*

_____ **D.** *The Lowly Liver*

_____ **E.** *Sabotage*

10. Gail Russell

_____ **A.** *Night Has a Thousand Eyes*

_____ **B.** *Cause for Alarm*

_____ **C.** *They Won't Believe Me*

_____ **D.** *The Uninvited*

_____ **E.** *The Tattered Dress*

11. Dick Powell

_____ **A.** *Murder My Sweet*

_____ **B.** *Johnny O'Clock*

_____ **C.** *Cornered*

_____ **D.** *To the Ends of the Earth*

_____ **E.** All of the above

12. Joan Crawford

_____ **A.** *Sudden Fear*

_____ **B.** *Nightmare*

_____ **C.** *Night Watch*

_____ **D.** *Above Suspicion*

_____ **E.** *Queen Bee*

13. Robert Cummings

_____ **A.** *Sleep My Love*

_____ **B.** *The Night of January 16th*

_____ **C.** *Slightly Honorable*

_____ **D.** *Dial M for Murder*

_____ **E.** *The Shutter Mysteries*

14. Ida Lupino

_____ **A.** *Out of the Fog*

_____ **B.** *The Adventures of Sherlock Holmes*

_____ **C.** *Woman in Hiding*

_____ **D.** *Beware, My Lovely*

_____ **E.** All of the above

15. Ingrid Bergman

_____ **A.** *Gaslight*

_____ **B.** *Spellbound*

_____ **C.** *Notorious*

_____ **D.** *Under Capricorn*

_____ **E.** All of the above

16. Humphrey Bogart

_____ **A.** *The Two Mrs. Carrolls*

_____ **B.** *The Gerber Kidnapping*

_____ **C.** *The Big Sleep*

_____ **D.** *The Maltese Falcon*

_____ **E.** All of the above

17. Edward G. Robinson

_____ **A.** *Double Indemnity*

_____ **B.** *The Woman in the Window*

_____ **C.** *Strangers on a Train*

_____ **D.** *The Glass Web*

_____ **E.** None of the above

18. Claude Rains

_____ **A.** *I Dreamed of Charlotte Brontë*

_____ **B.** *Fallen Sparrow*

_____ **C.** *The Unsuspected*

_____ **D.** *The Mystery of Edwin Drood*

_____ **E.** *When It Murders It Pours*

19. Ella Raines

_____ **A.** *Mudslide*

_____ **B.** *Phantom Lady*

_____ **C.** *The Suspect*

_____ **D.** *Enter Arsène Lupin*

_____ **E.** *Uncle Harry*

20. Laurence Olivier

_____ **A.** *The Last of Mrs. Cheyne*

_____ **B.** *The Mystery of the Tower*

_____ **C.** *Sleuth*

_____ **D.** *The Champagne Murders*

_____ **E.** *Rebecca*

21. James Mason

_____ **A.** *Bricks and Sticks*

_____ **B.** *Fallen Angel*

_____ **C.** *The Man in the Gray Velvet Suit*

_____ **D.** *Odd Man Out*

_____ **E.** *The Last of Sheila*

22. Joan Fontaine

_____ **A.** *Jealousy*

_____ **B.** *Ivy*

_____ **C.** *Suspicion*

_____ **D.** *The Notorious Landlady*

_____ **E.** *Terror at Trevi*

23. Alan Ladd and Veronica Lake

_____ **A.** *The Blue Dahlia*

_____ **B.** *Double Exposure*

_____ **C.** *My Nephew Drowned*

_____ **D.** *The Glass Key*

_____ **E.** *This Gun for Hire*

24. Gene Tierney

_____ **A.** *Whirlpool*

_____ **B.** *Black Widow*

_____ **C.** *Laura*

_____ **D.** *Leave Her to Heaven*

_____ **E.** None of the above

25. George Sanders

_____ **A.** *The Saint in London*

_____ **B.** *The Falcon's Brother*

_____ **C.** *Witness to Murder*

_____ **D.** *The Whole Truth*

_____ **E.** *Hangover Square*

26. Ann Baxter

_____ **A.** *Woman on the Ferry*

_____ **B.** *Who Killed Charlie's Aunt?*

_____ **C.** *The Blue Gardenia*

_____ **D.** *Adam's Madam*

_____ **E.** *Murder Will Out*

27. Basil Rathbone

_____ **A.** *Murders in the Rue Morgue*

_____ **B.** *The Hound of the Baskervilles*

_____ **C.** *Fingers at the Window*

_____ **D.** *Above Suspicion*

_____ **E.** *Suspicion*

28. Sydney Greenstreet

_____ **A.** *The Woman in White*

_____ **B.** *Voice of Merrill*

_____ **C.** *The Velvet Touch*

_____ **D.** *The Maltese Falcon*

_____ **E.** *The Mask of Dimitrios*

29. Richard Widmark

_____ **A.** *Don't Bother to Knock*

_____ **B.** *Kiss of Death*

_____ **C.** *A Woman's Vengeance*

_____ **D.** *The Long Goodbye*

_____ **E.** *He Who Laughs Last*

30. Barbara Stanwyck

_____ **A.** *Dragonwyck*

_____ **B.** *Murder in Flatbush*

_____ **C.** *Dark Mirror*

_____ **D.** *Sorry, Wrong Number*

_____ **E.** *I Confess*

IT CAN ONLY BE . . .

Match the clues on the left with the movie titles on the right. Score 4 points for each correct answer.

_____	**1.** Jukebox syndicate	**A.**	*Topkapi*
_____	**2.** Lipstick coated with phosphorous	**B.**	*The Power of the Whistler*
_____	**3.** "We may be rats, crooks, and murderers . . . but we're Americans."	**C.**	*The Stranger*
		D.	*The Crime Doctor's Diary*
_____	**4.** Poisoned birthday cake	**E.**	*Quiet, Please, Murder*
_____	**5.** Heroin hidden in a doll	**F.**	*Wait Until Dark*
_____	**6.** Jeweled dagger	**G.**	*Philo Vance's Gamble*
_____	**7.** Fixation with clocks	**H.**	*Seven Miles from Alcatraz*
_____	**8.** Butterflies		
_____	**9.** Brooklyn hoods	**I.**	*The City Across the River*
_____	**10.** Shakespeare forgeries	**J.**	*The Collector*

SCORING

Crime on the Silver Screen   _____

Chandler on Film   _____

The Barrymore Gang   _____

Grant's Leading Ladies   _____

Actors in Series   _____

Modus Operandi   _____

Femmes Fatales   _____

Death at 16 Frames per Second   _____

A Title Spelled
   "B-O-X O-F-F-I-C-E"   _____

Leading Men and Women   _____

It Can Only Be . . .   _____

Chapter Total Score   _____

The Verdict

If you scored between 532 and 348   You can—and do—find most of your perpetrators in dark rooms.

If you scored between 347 and 174   Watch the Late Show more often.

If you scored between 173 and 0   Chances are you go to bed before the late news.

COPS ON

THE BOX

*It should be possible . . . to write a detective
story in which the detective was recognizable
as a human being.*

— E.C. BENTLEY

In the late 1940s Hollywood began to turn up its nose at
the mystery, and to this date most filmmakers have not
reconsidered this snub. Television, though, took up the
slack. From *Dragnet* to *Hill Street Blues*, television pro-
ducers have managed to supply mystery lovers with
enough new material to force us to keep our TV sets in
good repair.

Through the years, all of our favorite types of
mysteries have been presented to us on television. We've
seen every kind of police procedural. The antihero, in the
form of Columbo and Rockford, has emerged full-blown
on television. Even Modesty Blaise had a short run in the
sixties.

We would also like to give a nod to Public Broad-
casting in America, which has presented such delights as
the "Mystery" series and lengthy series based on
mystery/suspense works, such as John le Carré's "*Tinker,
Tailor, Soldier, Spy.*"

Overall, the marriage between TV and the mystery
has been a good one. And judging from the best-seller
lists and bookstore shelves, the printed word is none the
worse for it.

MURDER IN YOUR LIVING ROOM

Score 4 points for each correct answer.

1. In which series did actor Craig Stevens play a television detective who frequented a jazz club called Mother's?

   _____ **A.** *Peter Gunn*

   _____ **B.** *Racket Squad*

   _____ **C.** *Columbo*

   _____ **D.** *Hawaiian Eye*

2. Which actor played a plainclothesman operating out of Chicago in *M Squad*?

   _____ **A.** Richard Boone

   _____ **B.** Pat Boone

   _____ **C.** Lee Marvin

   _____ **D.** Lee Majors

3. David Janssen played a private eye in which TV series?

   _____ **A.** *Topaz*

   _____ **B.** *Edmund Carat*

   _____ **C.** *All That Glitters Is Not Gould*

   _____ **D.** *Richard Diamond*

4. What was the name of the private detective employed by Perry Mason?

_____ **A.** Captain Braddock

_____ **B.** Paul Drake

_____ **C.** Alicia van Helsing

_____ **D.** Mike Barnett

5. Vanessa, played by Yvette Mimieux, is a criminologist in which TV series?

_____ **A.** *Vanessa Loves a Mystery*

_____ **B.** *Pete and Gladys*

_____ **C.** *The Most Deadly Game*

_____ **D.** *Police Story*

6. Who are the two detectives in *Hawaiian Eye*?

_____ **A.** Malloy and Reed

_____ **B.** Dickens and Fenster

_____ **C.** Halloran and Muldoon

_____ **D.** Lopaka and Steele

7. Who played Nick Charles in the TV series *The Thin Man*?

_____ **A.** Martin Milner

_____ **B.** Pierre Salinger

_____ **C.** Richard Denning

_____ **D.** Peter Lawford

8. Who played Mrs. North in the *Mr. and Mrs. North* TV series?

   _____ **A.** Barbara Britton

   _____ **B.** Anne Jeffries

   _____ **C.** Myrna Loy

   _____ **D.** Dorothy Collins

9. Frank Lovejoy starred as a TV good guy in which series?

   _____ **A.** *I Spy*

   _____ **B.** *Omnibus*

   _____ **C.** *Meet McGraw*

   _____ **D.** *Streets of Cincinnati*

10. What famous mystery writer created the TV series *Checkmate*?

   _____ **A.** Dashiell Hammett

   _____ **B.** Eric Ambler

   _____ **C.** Bobby Fisher

   _____ **D.** Agatha Christie

11. In which city is the series *The 87th Precinct* set?

   _____ **A.** London

   _____ **B.** New York

   _____ **C.** Chicago

   _____ **D.** Des Moines

12. Ben Gazzara plays a detective in which of the following crime series?

_____ A. *Arrest and Trial*

_____ B. *Cease and Desist*

_____ C. *The Blue Knight*

_____ D. *Run for Your Life*

13. The TV movie *Prescription Murder* was the pilot for which popular police series?

_____ A. *McMillan and Wife*

_____ B. *McCloud*

_____ C. *Charlie's Angels*

_____ D. *Columbo*

14. Who narrated the long-running gangster series *The Untouchables*?

_____ A. George Putnam

_____ B. Hugh Downs

_____ C. Walter Winchell

_____ D. Snookie Lanson

15. What is Banacek's ethnic origin?

_____ A. Greek

_____ B. Turkish

_____ C. Finnish

_____ D. Polish

16. In *Hart to Hart,* who plays the sidekick?

_____ **A.** Lionel Stander

_____ **B.** Anthony Zerbe

_____ **C.** Nancy Walker

_____ **D.** David Doyle

17. Lee Horsley plays a hardworking sidekick in which TV series?

_____ **A.** *Hill Street Blues*

_____ **B.** *White Shadow*

_____ **C.** *Nero Wolfe*

_____ **D.** *Quincy*

COPS OR PI'S

The following TV good guys are either working cops or private eyes. Mark each C for Cop or P for Private Eye. Score 3 points for each correct answer.

1. Mike Barnett   _____

2. Boston Blackie   _____

3. Pepper Anderson   _____

4. Fabian   _____

5. Kookie   _____

6. McGarrett   _____

7. Mike Shayne   _____

8. Francis Muldoon   _____

9. Harry Orwell   _____

10. Jim Rockford   _____

PROFESSIONS

Not all detectives are private eyes. The professions on the left are practiced by the major sleuths of the TV series on the right. Match them up. (Some professions apply to more than one series.) Score 4 points for each correct answer.

_____ **1.** Journalism

_____ **2.** Medicine

_____ **3.** Insurance investigation

_____ **4.** Lawyer

A. *Quincy*

B. *Longstreet*

C. *Big Town*

D. *Banacek*

E. *Name of the Game*

F. *Owen Marshall*

MURDER, U.S.A.

Match the locales on the left with the TV series on the right. (Some locales apply to more than one series.) Score 3 points for each correct answer.

_____ **1.** Miami Beach

_____ **2.** New Orleans

_____ **3.** New York City

_____ **4.** Los Angeles

_____ **5.** San Francisco

_____ **6.** Beverly Hills

_____ **7.** Boston

_____ **8.** Pasadena

A. *Banacek*

B. *The New Breed*

C. *77 Sunset Strip*

D. *McMillan and Wife*

E. *Bourbon Street*

F. *Adam-12*

G. *Naked City*

H. *Ironside*

I. *Surfside 6*

J. *The Snoop Sisters*

GREAT MYSTERY SERIES

Match the clues on the left with the TV series on the right. Score 4 points for each correct answer.

_____ **1.** Cricket

_____ **2.** The Charleston Club

_____ **3.** Sebastion Cabot

_____ **4.** Lieutenant Guthrie

_____ **5.** "Ten-Four"

_____ **6.** Mary Tyler Moore's legs

_____ **7.** The Crescendo

_____ **8.** Badge 714

_____ **9.** Joseph Wambaugh

_____ **10.** Troy Donahue

A. *Checkmate*

B. *Richard Diamond*

C. *Highway Patrol*

D. *Dragnet*

E. *Police Story*

F. *Hawaiian Eye*

G. *Lineup*

H. *Staccato*

I. *The Roaring Twenties*

J. *Surfside 6*

THE FACTS OF THE MATTER

Are the following questions True or False? Score 4 points for each correct answer.

1. TV good guy Staccato played the trumpet in a Greenwich Village club. True or False?

2. J.R., the assistant to Barnaby Jones, is related to Jones. True or False?

3. Mannix's first name is Manny. True or False?

4. Julie, Linc, and Pete are the three police assistants to Chief Ironside. True or False?

5. Longstreet's first name is Jack. True or False?

6. Kent Taylor starred in the TV series *Boston Blackie*. True or False?

7. Holbrook, Ballard, and Russo are characters in the TV series *The Detectives*. True or False?

8. Lee Remick played Mrs. Charles in the TV series *The Thin Man*. True or False?

9. Karl Malden and Michael Douglas starred in *Naked City*. True or False?

10. The TV series *The Untouchables* was set mainly in Philadelphia. True or False?

THE MOSTEST

We know opinion varies as to which sleuth is most handsome, beautiful, clever, and interesting, and we have had long and unresolved discussions on these matters. However, you should have very little difficulty matching the sleuths on the left with the characteristics on the right. Score 2 points for each correct answer.

_____	1. Ellery Queen	**A.** Fattest
_____	2. Baretta	**B.** Most annoying—a real *noodge*
_____	3. Cannon	
_____	4. Columbo	**C.** Thinnest
_____	5. Jim Rockford	**D.** Most underpaid
		E. Flakiest

WELL OFF OR HARD UP?

Just because you work for the police doesn't mean you have to be poor. And just because you're in private practice doesn't necessarily mean you're rich. Mark W for Well Off and H for Hard Up next to each of these TV good guys. Score 2 points for each correct answer.

1. Amos Burke   _____

2. Jim Rockford   _____

3. Nick and Nora Charles   _____

4. The Saint   _____

5. John Steed   _____

6. Harry O _____

7. Michael Shayne _____

8. Columbo _____

9. Meet McGraw _____

10. McMillan _____

SCORING

Murder in Your Living Room _____

Cops or PI's _____

Professions _____

Murder, U.S.A. _____

Great Mystery Series _____

The Facts of the Matter _____

The Mostest _____

Well Off or Hard Up _____

　Chapter Total Score _____

The Verdict

If you scored between 262 and 175　You cried when they took *Rockford* off the air.

If you scored between 174 and 87　You may watch a lot of prime time, but you're missing some important reruns.

If you scored between 86 and 0　Get your set fixed.

LITTLE-KNOWN

FACTS ABOUT

THE AUTHORS

If I'm not having fun writing a book, no one's going to have any fun reading it.

— REX STOUT

In the mid-1970s, a novel was published entitled *Hammet*. The work made use of the fascinating details of that mystery writer's life and proved what many mystery readers had known for years—that the lives of mystery authors are often as fascinating as the characters and plots they create.

Many mystery writers have had to make their living in unusual occupations, supporting themselves while they worked on the books we have come to love. Conversely, great mystery novels have come from authors who never fancied themselves writers but developed fine tales out of their experiences.

Other authors have created persons for themselves, and have come to be identified with particular classes of people and areas of the country. When these authors become too well identified with a particular genre, they often turn to a pseudonym to liberate themselves from their readers' demands.

The following quizzes will test your knowledge of mystery writers and their unique world.

BY NIGHT, A MYSTERY WRITER. BY DAY . . .

Many of our favorite authors have, through either necessity or desire, occupied themselves with work other than writing mystery novels. Identify the other occupation for each of the following authors. Score 4 points for each correct answer.

1. Dorothy L. Sayers

    _____ **A.** Medieval scholar

    _____ **B.** Opera singer

    _____ **C.** English teacher

    _____ **D.** Epicene

2. Raymond Chandler

    _____ **A.** Evangelist

    _____ **B.** Minor-league baseball player

    _____ **C.** Bootlegger

    _____ **D.** Oil company executive

3. Dorothy Uhnak

    _____ **A.** New York City cop

    _____ **B.** Missionary

    _____ **C.** Photographer

    _____ **D.** Actress

4. Dashiell Hammett

_____ **A.** Book salesman

_____ **B.** Pinkerton man

_____ **C.** Physicist

_____ **D.** Wine taster

5. Josephine Bell

_____ **A.** Physician

_____ **B.** Legal secretary

_____ **C.** Stewardess

_____ **D.** Telephone operator

6. Josephine Tey

_____ **A.** Gym teacher

_____ **B.** Ballerina

_____ **C.** Intelligence agent

_____ **D.** Waitress

7. Joyce Porter

_____ **A.** Member of Parliament

_____ **B.** Bus driver

_____ **C.** RAF officer

_____ **D.** Reporter

The joy—or perhaps the money—in mystery writing is evidenced in some families that have more than one contributor to the crime fiction field. Score 4 points for every correct answer.

8. Margaret Millar's husband is also a well-known crime novelist. Can you identify him?

_____ **A.** Rae Foley

_____ **B.** Ellery Queen

_____ **C.** Ross Macdonald

_____ **D.** John D. MacDonald

9. Ursula Curtiss followed in the footsteps of her famous mystery-writing mother. Who is her mother?

_____ **A.** Helen Reilly

_____ **B.** Ruby Keeler

_____ **C.** Agatha Christie

_____ **D.** Patricia Wentworth

10. Choose the correct relationship between Manfred B. Lee and Frederick Dannay, alias Ellery Queen.

_____ **A.** Father and son

_____ **B.** Cousins

_____ **C.** Brothers

_____ **D.** Uncle and nephew

11. Margaret Cole collaborated with her husband, G. D. H. Cole, on a number of mystery novels. Her brother was also a contributor to the crime fiction profession. Can you identify him?

_____ **A.** Raymond Postgate

_____ **B.** Nat King Cole

_____ **C.** Gore Vidal

_____ **D.** Colin Watson

12. Martin Beck is the dour detective in a series by Maj Sjowall and Per Wahloo. Maj and Per were related in what way?

_____ **A.** No way at all

_____ **B.** Sisters

_____ **C.** Wife and husband

_____ **D.** Sister and brother

Some dabblers in the mystery field are better known for their work in other professions. Score 4 points for every correct answer.

13. *The President's Mystery* is a novel based on a plot idea by which American president?

_____ **A.** Franklin D. Roosevelt

_____ **B.** Theodore Roosevelt

_____ **C.** Lyndon B. Johnson

_____ **D.** Calvin Coolidge

14. A famous author of children's books also wrote mysteries, such as *The Red House Mystery, A Table Near the Band,* and *Murder at Eleven.* Who is the writer?

_____ **A.** L. Frank Baum

_____ **B.** Margaret O'Brien

_____ **C.** Lewis Carroll

_____ **D.** A. A. Milne

15. Which mystery writer served as an economic adviser to President Franklin D. Roosevelt?

_____ **A.** Frances Perkins

_____ **B.** Harry Hopkins

_____ **C.** A. H. Z. Carr

_____ **D.** Huey P. Long

PSEUDONYMS AND ALIASES

Did you ever finish a book by an author you just discovered, only to learn that he or she was a long-time favorite of yours simply writing under a pseudonym?

You shouldn't have been surprised. For a variety of reasons, many writers in the crime fiction field use a pseudonym.

Match the authors and their aliases. Score 3 points for each correct answer.

_____ **1.** A. A. Fair

_____ **2.** Kenneth Millar

_____ **3.** Edgar Box

_____ **4.** Carter Dickson

_____ **5.** Harry Longbough

_____ **6.** Elizabeth MacKintosh

_____ **7.** J. I. M. Stewart

_____ **8.** C. Day Lewis

_____ **9.** David Cornwall

_____ **10.** Ellery Queen

A. Gore Vidal

B. Erle Stanley Gardner

C. John Dickson Carr

D. Ross Macdonald

E. William Goldman

F. Michael Innes

G. Josephine Tey

H. John le Carré

I. Barnaby Ross

J. Nicholas Blake

TELLTALE PARAGRAPHS

Mystery writers have a modus operandi, just like their heroes and villains. Authors are often identifiable not only by their style but also by their subject matter and atmosphere. See if you can choose the right authors after reading the brief excerpts below.

Score 6 points for each correct answer.

1.　　　He managed to smile at her. "I know this sounds silly," he said, "but where did we meet?"

"Downstairs in the lobby," she said. "You were trying to steal the lilies from the flower display to take upstairs as a present to the most beautiful girl in the world, and the room clerk was being a little difficult about it. You looked sort of helpless, so we adopted you."

"Oh," Dennis Morrison said. He looked down at the rug. "I don't know what you think of me, doing a thing like this, on my wedding night."

"Think nothing of it," ＿＿ said. "On our wedding night, ＿＿ was in jail for reckless driving."

"And assaulting an officer in the attempt to do his duty," ＿＿ said proudly. "The next night, ＿＿ got mixed up with some Southern moonshine and didn't get home for eighteen hours."

＿＿＿＿ **A.** Collin Wilcox, *The Third Victim*

＿＿＿＿ **B.** Lionel Black, *Two Ladies in Verona*

＿＿＿＿ **C.** Sebastien Japrisot, *Trap for Cinderella*

＿＿＿＿ **D.** Craig Rice, *Having Wonderful Crime*

2.　　　"Now and then I receive the impression that you suspect me of neglecting this or that detail of our business. Ordinarily you are wrong, which is as it should be. In the labyrinth of any problem that confronts us, we must select the most promising paths; if we attempt to

follow all at once we shall arrive nowhere. In any
art—and I am an artist or nothing—one of the deepest
secrets of excellence is a discerning elimination. Of
course that is a truism."

"Yes, sir."

"Yes. Take the art of writing. I am, let us say, describ-
ing the actions of my hero rushing to greet his beloved,
who has just entered the forest. *He sprang up from the log
on which he had been sitting, with his left foot forward; as
he did so, one leg of his trousers fell properly into place
but the other remained hitched up at the knee. He began
running towards her, first his right foot, then his left, then
his right again, then left, right, left, right, left, right . . .* As
you see, some of that can surely be left out—indeed, must
be, if he is to accomplish his welcoming embrace in the
same chapter. So the artist must leave out vastly more
than he puts in, and one of his chief cares is to leave out
nothing vital to his work."

_____ **A.** Arthur Conan Doyle, *The Red-Headed
League*

_____ **B.** Rex Stout, *The League of Frightened
Men*

_____ **C.** Carter Dickson, *Behind the Crimson
Blind*

_____ **D.** Richard Forrest, *A Child's Garden of
Death*

3.   The mosquitoes had welted us abundantly, but I
knew the evidence would disappear quickly. There is a
kind of semiimmunity you acquire if you live long
enough in mosquito country. The itch is caused by the
blood-thinner they inject, so they can suck the mixed
fluids up their narrow snouts. But the redbug bites are
something else. No immunity there. We both had them
from ankles to groin. The itch of the chigger bite lasts so
long that the mythology says they lay eggs under the skin.
Not so. It is a very savage itch, and the only way to cut the

weeks down to a few days is to use any preparation con-
taining a nerve-deadening agent, along with a cortisone
spray. The sun warmed us and began to dry the money.
More cars and trucks began to barrel through with
fading Doppler whine. A flock of ground doves policed
the area. I scratched the chigger bites and thought of a
big deep bed with clean white sheets.

_____ **A.** Roy Vickers, *The Enemy Within*

_____ **B.** Gordon Ashe, *Death in the Trees*

_____ **C.** Shelly Smith, *Lord Have Mercy*

_____ **D.** John D. MacDonald, *The Long Lavendar Look*

4.　　　　I don't know what would happen if women started
taking their husbands' advice, but I know what wouldn't
have happened if I'd taken Tom's. I wouldn't have gone to
Natchez for the Garden Club Pilgrimage, not with
Cornelia Cartwright and Letty Drayton anyway. I
wouldn't, moreover, have had my picture in every
newspaper in the country as friend of the murdered club
woman. Nor would I have had to explain the headlines
"Doctor's Wife Reveals Hidden Love" to everybody who
assumed it was *my* hidden love—including, for one pret-
ty uncomfortable moment, Tom himself. It did have one
advantage, however. Everybody in town developed sudden and inexplicable ailments and rushed to the office, so
that we're putting the new wing on the house this year in-
stead of next. All things being equal, I think we'd rather
have waited.

_____ **A.** Leslie Ford, *Murder with Southern Hospitality*

_____ **B.** Francis Beeding, *Death Walks in Eastrepps*

_____ **C.** Edgar Wallace, *Beyond Recall*

_____ **D.** Mignon G. Eberhart, *Murder by an Aristocrat*

5.   I sat near her on the carpeted floor, which repeated the design of the stained-glass window. There were times when I almost wished I was a priest. I was growing weary of other people's pain and wondered if a black suit and a white collar might serve as armor against it. I'd never know. My grandmother in Contra Costa County had marked me for the priesthood, but I had slipped away under the fence.

Looking into Paola's opaque black eyes, I thought that the grief you shared with women was most always partly desire. At least sometimes you could take them to bed, I thought, and exchange a temporary kindness, which priests were denied. But not Paola. Both she and the woman at Sycamore Point belonged to dead men tonight. Chapel thoughts.

_____ **A.** Richard S. Prather, *Darling, It's Death*

_____ **B.** Leonore Offord, *The Glass Mask*

_____ **C.** Ross Macdonald, *The Blue Hammer*

_____ **D.** Dashiell Hammett, *Woman in the Dark*

JOHN D. MACDONALD— SHOWING HIS TRUE COLORS

The hues and tints used by John D. MacDonald in his titles have become a trademark of the colorful Travis McGee mysteries. Find the colors on the right to complete the titles on the left. Score 3 points for each correct answer.

_____	1. *The Quick _____ Fox*	**A.** *Pink*
_____	2. *A _____ Place for Dying*	**B.** *Crimson*
_____	3. *Bright _____ for the Shroud*	**C.** *Gray*
		D. *Orange*
_____	4. *One Fearful _____ Eye*	**E.** *Indigo*
_____	5. *Pale _____ for Guilt*	**F.** *Red*
_____	6. *The _____ Ruse*	**G.** *Green*
_____	7. *The _____ Ripper*	**H.** *Purple*
_____	8. *The Girl in the Plain _____ Wrapper*	**I.** *Scarlet*
		J. *Gold*
_____	9. *Deadly Shade of _____*	**K.** *Brown*
_____	10. *Free Fall in _____*	**L.** *Yellow*
_____	11. *Nightmare in _____*	
_____	12. *Dress Her in _____*	

EIGHT BY-THE-WAY BY LINES

Mystery writers aren't always best known for their crime fiction. Score 5 points for every correct name you uncover.

1. Thriller writers Gordon Davis, John Baxter, Robert Dietrich, and David St. John are all which one of the following?

    _____ **A.** Robert Heinlein, science fiction writer

    _____ **B.** Willie Shoemaker, three-time Kentucky Derby winner

    _____ **C.** E. Howard Hunt, White House consultant to President Richard M. Nixon

    _____ **D.** C. S. Forester, the creator of Horatio Hornblower

2. Mario Cleri, who wrote the spy thriller *Six Graves to Munich*, is also known as which of the following?

    _____ **A.** Gunter Grass

    _____ **B.** Mario Puzo

    _____ **C.** Edward Albee

    _____ **D.** George Patton

3. Robert L. Pike and A. C. Lamprey are pseudonyms for which of the following?

    _____ **A.** Salmon P. Chase

    _____ **B.** Sidney Hook

    _____ **C.** Robert Fish

    _____ **D.** Sam Bass

4. *The President Vanishes*, a pseudonymously published mystery novel, was really written by which of the following?

_____ **A.** Gerald Ford

_____ **B.** James Hilton

_____ **C.** Mary McMullen

_____ **D.** Rex Stout

5. Gothic mystery writer A. M. Barnard's more famous identity has only recently been discovered, and the stories—more than 100 years old—are now being reprinted. Who was A. M. Barnard?

_____ **A.** Marie Curie

_____ **B.** Ulysses S. Grant

_____ **C.** Thomas Burke

_____ **D.** Louisa May Alcott

6. He published his first story at age thirteen, entitled "The Mystery of the Raymond Mortgage." His later works were great contributions to literature, but not in the mystery genre. Who is he?

_____ **A.** F. Scott Fitzgerald

_____ **B.** William Faulkner

_____ **C.** Truman Capote

_____ **D.** Raymond Postgate

7. Which dramatist and essayist wrote a mystery novel turned film entitled *The Old Dark House*?

_____ **A.** George Bernard Shaw

_____ **B.** J. B. Priestly

_____ **C.** Voltaire

_____ **D.** Kurt Vonnegut

8. Which of the following lived a life of crime before helping to found the Police de Sûreté in France, opening his own detective agency, and publishing accounts* of his interesting life on both sides of the law?

_____ **A.** Rabelais

_____ **B.** Zola

_____ **C.** Vidocq

_____ **D.** Marten Cumberland

FOOTPRINT

*which may have been ghostwritten.

SCORING

By Night, a Mystery Writer,
　By Day . . .　　　　　　　　　　　_____

Pseudonyms and Aliases　　　　_____

Telltale Paragraphs　　　　　　_____

John D. MacDonald Showing
　His True Colors　　　　　　　_____

Eight By-the-Way Bylines　　　_____

　Chapter Total Score　　　　_____

THE VERDICT

**If you scored
between 206 and 158**　　Your library of mysteries is probably a national resource.

**If you scored
between 157 and 131**　　Broaden your interests — read a few new authors.

**If you scored
between 130 and 0**　　C'mon! You're not even reading the book jackets!

MISCELLANEOUS MAYHEM

We tried to stop the book right here. But one good question deserves another, and we ended up with a whole new section of quizzes.

No doubt the questions in this book have led you to think, "But what about so-and-so? He's my favorite mystery writer, and I haven't seen one question about him." So write to us! If we get the chance to update, revise, or do a sequel to *The Mystery Reader's Quiz Book*, we'd be happy to have your suggestions.

READ ALL ABOUT IT!

This quiz tests your dedication to the mystery genre (or your age) with some questions about the evolution of this literary form. The facts come from the Haycraft-Queen Definitive Library of Detective-Crime-Mystery Fiction (Biblo and Tannen, N.Y., N.Y., 1974).

Match the newspaper headlines on the left with the mystery writers and titles on the right. Score 2 points for every correct answer.

_____ 1. *News Item*
PATERNITY SUIT
LOOMS—IS E.A. THE
REAL FATHER?

_____ 2. *Obituary*
PLOT GOES TO
LITERARY GIANT'S
GRAVE

_____ 3. *Fashion News*
IN THIS
SEASON—VERY PALE
TONES AND
SEMIPRECIOUS
STONES

_____ 4. *Police Blotter*
CRIME WAVE HALTED
BY EX-CON

_____ 5. *Travel Section*
MAKING THE CASE
FOR KANSAS

_____ 6. *Home Section*
NEWEST INTERIOR
DESIGN HINT—DO
YOUR DEN IN RED

_____ 7. *Financial News*
THE NEW
ADMINISTRATION IS
PUTTING THE BITE ON
THE LITTLE GUY

A. Earl Derr Biggers, *The House Without a Key*

B. Louis Joseph Vance, *The Lone Wolf*

C. Mary Roberts Rinehart, *The Circular Staircase*

D. Roy Vickers, *The Department of Dead Ends*

E. Raymond Chandler, *The Big Sleep*

F. Daphne du Maurier, *Rebecca*

G. Arthur Conan Doyle, *A Study in Scarlet*

H. Charles Dickens, *The Mystery of Edwin Drood*

I. Edgar Allan Poe, *Tales*

J. H. F. Heard, *A Taste for Honey*

_____ 8. *Home Section*
ARCHITECTS GOING
ROUND IN CIRCLES
OVER UPS AND
DOWNS IN STYLES

_____ 9. *Editorial Page*
PATIENTS
ISOLATED — NURSING
HOME REFORMS
DEMANDED

_____ 10. *Want Ads*
TO LET —
BACHELOR QUARTERS
AVAILABLE

_____ 11. *News Item*
SOLITARY CARNIVORE
STALKING CITY

_____ 12. *Book Review*
"FOUL PLAY" CRY
CRITICS AT NEWEST
WHODUNIT

_____ 13. *Medical News*
INSIDERS ARE
CHORTLING OVER
PATHOLOGY DEPT.'S
WHIMSICAL QUESTION

_____ 14. *Home Safety Hints*
POLICE HAVE ANSWER
TO RISING CRIME
RATE IN OUR
SUBURBS

K. Agatha Christie, *The Murder of Roger Ackroyd*

L. Dorothy L. Sayers, *Whose Body*

M. Wilkie Collins, *The Woman in White; The Moonstone*

N. Ellery Queen, *The Roman Hat Mystery*

O. Cornell Woolrich, *The Phantom Lady*

P. Anna Katherine Green, *The Leavenworth Case*

Q. Mrs. Belloc Lowndes, *The Lodger*

R. James M. Cain, *The Postman Always Rings Twice*

S. Rufus King, *Murder by the Clock*

T. Baroness Orczy, *The Old Man in the Corner*

U. Emile Gaboriau, *Le Dossier No. 113*

V. Bram Stoker, *Dracula*

_____ **15.** *Fashion Item*
DACHÉ WANTS
QUOTA ON IMPORTS

_____ **16.** *Real Estate Section*
FIRE SALE—LARGE
ESTATE AVAILABLE—REASONABLE

_____ **17.** *News Item*
ENCEPHALITIS OUT-
BREAK REPORTED

_____ **18.** *Funnies*
WHO WAS THAT
WOMAN I SAW YOU
WITH LAST NIGHT?

_____ **19.** *Food Section*
TRY THIS NATURAL
FOOD FOR YOUR
SWEET TOOTH

_____ **20.** *Political News*
COUNCILWOMAN COMPLAINS—
COMMITTEE HAS
BEEN SITTING TOO
LONG

_____ **21.** *Society Section*
MEETING SCHEDULED
AT BILTMORE

_____ **22.** *Letters to the Editor*
WHY ISN'T MY MAIL
DELIVERED MORE
THAN ONCE A DAY
WITH THIS NEW
POSTAGE INCREASE?

HIDDENHEREAREBOTHGOOD ANDBADGUYS

Find the hidden names for 3 points each. Answers may be first names, last names, or first and last names, spelled out diagonally (left to right), horizontally (left to right), or vertically (top to bottom).

```
H I D D E N H E R E A R E B O T H G O O D A N D B A D G U Y S
M B C E A H L A C X S R V E B A T H N Q U A I N R U E V B C A
C J U F P G R W N K O P U N E X J O S E D A S I L V A M F S T
O A J E B A A E C A D O Y C I M R T E B L R C T O M N U I C U
L N X L C H R F I L U R G O L J E E W R M O R I A R T Y N E R
D R A B I A L T L X V D F L A M B E A U P V E H S B E A Y T N
R V C R U M I O M U Y B D I G L K Z R Q B E H R E N S R P X I
Y A L C J B E R A E N B O N A P A R T E E G J V C U S C E S N
N R A E A L G N I S N A A N L E R X J O A Q U I N H A W K S J
S E N R N E B S P E C T R E R E L D L N O B C L P D F L N J N
T V Y D C D U J L E V E Z M V I A U T D N S C O E B H P A U A
E Q A R Z O K Q E R S B E R T R A M L Y N C H R T R B H E D O
M A R T I N B E C K J P B H U B G E F A T H M N E C O Y L G P
Y C D S S P B L O F E L D A M E L O G D U A I R R G L U D E S
L W C I S A F W Q M V E O C O C K R I L L F Q U S D O V X D T
A L N C A R L V O N G R O O T E L C A Y V I M M O I F D S E M
I N T E R N A T I O N A L C O P S C R O O K S A N D S P I E S
```

DIAGONAL

Counterespionage arm of British intelligence

The Sûreté sleuth from *They Wouldn't Be Chessmen* and *The House in Lordship Lane*

Graham Greene's Harry

Capetown cop created by Peter Godfrey

HORIZONTAL

Works with the Brazilian Police and Interpol in such exotic settings as Rio, São Paulo, and the Amazon jungle

The "Napoleon of Crime," alleged to have fallen to his death from the Reichenbach Falls in Switzerland in a titanic battle with the Master of all sleuths

A notorious jewel thief who is pursued by Father Brown in *The Blue Cross;* in later Father Brown episodes he has turned good guy and assists in solving crimes

Michael Gilbert's British spy who enjoys beekeeping and chess

Australian police inspector with a historical name

An operative for the CIA in Southeast Asia, he is half Spanish, half American Indian

The worldwide network that conspires against both the Soviet Union and the United States in several Ian Fleming spy thrillers

John W. Vandercook's investigator for the League of Nations' Permanent Control Board

The cop in *The Man on the Balcony* and *The Man Who Went Up in Smoke*

Evil agent featured in *On Her Majesty's Secret Service* and *You Only Live Twice*

Sleuth featured in *What Dread Hand* and *Tour de Force* by Christianna Brand

Disguised as a Dutch curator, but really a dangerous German spy, created by Ernest Bramah

VERTICAL

Flamboyant and eccentric French police official sometimes referred to as "the most dangerous man in Europe"

H.R.F. Keating's expert at the Bombay CID.

First name of Commissaire Dax of the Paris Police Judiciare

Prominent member of British intelligence service, created by Manning Coles ("If a country is worth living in, it is worth fighting for.")

Master Soviet spy pursued by George Smiley

The Lone Wolf

Eric Ambler's Czechoslovakian refugee turned amateur sleuth

Emil Baboriau's bad guy turned good is a master of disguise

Japan's top secret agent's last name

Baghdad inspector's last name is his first name

Archenemy created by H. C. McNeille who in *The Final Count* is the mastermind behind a nearly successful plot to rule the world

He solved the mysteries of *The Chinese Lake Murders, The Chinese Maze Murders,* and *The Chinese Gold Murders*

LEAVE 'EM LAUGHING

Physically abused, psychologically strained, and deeply tired detectives sometimes exhaust us as well as themselves. It's a pleasure to be revitalized by books and movies that offer a bit of comic relief.

For each description, choose the book title and author. Score 4 points for each correct answer.

1. Members of a devout Sherlockian club are shocked to hear from the mouth of a fellow that the Master was really a pompous fool—further, that the deductive techniques utilized by Holmes are quite ineffective in the pursuit of real criminals. This malcontent insists he could vanish without hope of being found by anyone using these methods. This challenge is accepted by the True Believers, and a merry, if sometimes bizarre, chase ending in murder is run through the state of Pennsylvania. Although the villain is brought to justice, the price is very high—a woman is permitted to attend a meeting of the Sherlockian club!

   _____ **A.** *The Golden Swan Murder* by Dorothy Cameron Disney

   _____ **B.** *The Puzzle of the Silver Persian* by Stuart Palmer

   _____ **C.** *Death Is a Red Rose* by Dorothy Eden

   _____ **D.** *Copper Beeches* by Arthur Lewis

2. To a society of serious-minded aesthetes, the government has gone too far in raising the tax on theater seats. Nine members of the society decide to pursue all methods of redressing this philistine madness, until at last it is apparent that assassination is the

only reasonable course open to them. Much mayhem ensues, including the murder of the offending government official, until, with the objective accomplished, the leader of the group heads for New York to correct the ways of the United Nations.

_____ **A.** *The Fourteen Points* by Arthur B. Reeve

_____ **B.** *The Singular Case of the Multiple Dead* by Mark McShane

_____ **C.** *Death at the Bowl* by Raoul Whitfield

_____ **D.** *Assassins Have Starry Eyes* by Donald Hamilton

3. Headless bodies and vice versa keep the denizens of an English village in confusion until a professor on sabbatical sorts things out. Two independent murderers emerge in this tale of urgent sex and old-fashioned blackmail. Head switching, a missing arm, a cosh from a Nazi concentration camp, and a hideously noisy electrical transformer known as "the pisser" combine to boggle the minds of the authorities until it is discovered that one of their own is the guilty party. Sounds grim, but the list of eccentric characters and the mad situations in which they find themselves add up to a hilarious excursion through understated British comedy.

_____ **A.** *Adders on the Heath* by Gladys Mitchell

_____ **B.** *Trump for Alicia* by Joseph Mathewson

_____ **C.** *Glimpses of the Moon* by Edmond Crispin

_____ **D.** *The Deadly Percheron* by John Franklin Bardin

4. It has been said that cannibalism is addictive. Could that have been the motive for the murder of a stout,

seemingly harmless young woman? Our detective scoffs at the idea and settles for blackmail even though the evidence is remarkably thin. The villains are apprehended despite the laziness and incredible ineptitude of the sleuth. A woman explorer who had spent many years among cannibals and a former concentration camp victim prove to be the culprits. The remains of their victims, with a bit missing, are discovered neatly cut up in a deep freeze. So much for cannibalism. Or is it?

_____ **A.** *Dover One* by Joyce Porter

_____ **B.** *The Season of Danger* by Rosemary Gatesby

_____ **C.** *The Cannibal Who Overate* by Hugh Pentecost

_____ **D.** *Death Dines Out* by Theodore DuBois

5. A nasty-minded prankster finally gets his comeuppance for a death he was responsible for in the long-ago past. The entire town is notorious for its practical jokes. These tend to complicate the problems faced by the story's detective hero, but he is able to unravel the mystery of vengence in an explosively funny story that is tinged with pathos.

_____ **A.** *The Wedding Guest Sat on a Stone* by Richard Shattuck

_____ **B.** *Decoys* by Richard Hoyt

_____ **C.** *Bump in the Night* by Colin Watson

_____ **D.** *The Joker Deals with Death* by William Murdock Duncan

The following outlines may remind you of comic-mystery films you may have seen. Score 3 points for each correct answer.

6. A timid bank clerk determines to heist a huge supply of gold rather than face a penurious retirement. Organizing a gang to carry out this job provides some of the film's funniest moments. The Eiffel Tower is important for two reasons.

_____ **A.** *The Man on the Eiffel Tower*

_____ **B.** *The Lavender Hill Mob*

_____ **C.** *Larceny, Inc.*

_____ **D.** *The Green Man*

7. If our young heroine can prove she is sane, she will inherit the fortune of a murdered recluse. The emphasis is on comedy in this 1939 remake of a silent classic that itself was imported from the Broadway stage. This is one of the early old dark-house mysteries, with an abundance of secret passages and startling special effects.

_____ **A.** *The Cat and the Canary*

_____ **B.** *Guest in the House*

_____ **C.** *The Uninvited*

_____ **D.** *The Ladykillers*

8. Professional thieves are brought together for the purpose of stealing a precious stone that has religious significance to two African countries. A perfectly devised plan goes awry due to sweaty hands, but our intrepid heroes are nothing if not persistent. Our gallant band regroups and tries again—and again, and . . .

_____ **A.** *Topkapi*

_____ **B.** *The Italian Job*

_____ **C.** *The Hot Rock*

_____ **D.** *Big Deal on Madonna Street*

9. The detective hero pursues the naked truth. He confronts a roomful of suspects in order to trick the guilty party into giving himself or herself away. The bumbling (although relentless) questioning by the sleuth makes capture of the villain uncertain. The lights go out as planned, in the hope that the murderer will attempt to flee. A mad scramble ensues as all of the suspects try to escape. They all did it!

_____ **A.** *A Slight Case of Murder*

_____ **B.** *Whistling in the Dark*

_____ **C.** *A Shot in the Dark*

_____ **D.** *The Ex Mrs. Bradford*

10. An eccentric host invites several guests to his remote home and sets them a challenge they can't refuse. It will take more than one detective to solve the host's madcap mystery. Fortunately, many of the best sleuths are on hand. This provides them with an opportunity to display their differing styles. We wince —a bit—as we watch some of the best detective heroes stumble through the impossible plot.

_____ **A.** *It's a Mad Mad Mad Mad World*

_____ **B.** *Our Man in Havana*

_____ **C.** *Murder Most Foul*

_____ **D.** *Murder by Death*

TALL TALES

Who are we to criticize fishermen or golfers when we hear them report the size of the fish or the distance of the drive off the tee? Politeness requires us to be suitably impressed, even though we may nod knowingly to a third party at the first opportunity. It's a different story, however, when evildoers in a murder mystery attempt to mislead us with their tall tales.

We've come across some dandy abilis in our time, and if the truth be told, we've been fooled more than once. We sincerely appreciate the fact that older and wiser detectives are usually able to see through these fabrications to bring us to a solution.

Match the alibis to the books and films. Score 4 points for each correct answer. Note: There are more books and films listed than alibis. These are red herrings—which are essential to a good alibi.

A. *He Ran All the Way*   **F.** *Prescription: Murder*

B. *May You Die in Ireland*   **G.** *Swing, Swing Together*

C. *A Coat of Varnish*   **H.** *Double Indemnity*

D. *Tragedy of Law*   **I.** *Strangers on a Train*

E. *Strangers in 7A*   **J.** *Malice Aforethought*

_____ **1.** It's absurd to think his wife killed him, for she had saved his life in three recent murder attempts. Not true: These attempts were fakes that she devised for her own clever reasons.

_____ **2.** He couldn't have pushed her husband off a train. He was home working when the murder took place. Several people spoke to him on the phone that night. Not true: He had just enough time between phone calls to commit the murder and put the body near the railroad tracks.

_____ **3.** This doctor couldn't have given his wife an overdose of morphia, because his mistress was talking to him a good distance from the scene of the crime when the death took place. Not true: He had convinced his mistress her watch was fifteen minutes fast, which accounted for the time discrepancy.

_____ **4.** The apparent wife of a doctor stages an argument and leaves him aboard a plane departing
for Mexico. He couldn't have killed her, for she
was still alive and seen by the plane's passengers just before the plane took off with him on
it. Not true: The doctor's wife was already
strangled when his actress lover, disguised as
his wife, staged the argument.

_____ **5.** There is absolute proof that Guy did not
murder his wife, nor Charles his father. Both
men were far removed from the scene of the
crime when each murder took place. True:
They switched roles and places, which left the
police with apparent motiveless crimes.

SPOT THE RED·HERRING

Three of the books listed below were written by the
author indicated; one was written by someone else.
Score 2 points each for spotting the book that was not
written by the listed author, and 3 bonus points for
knowing who wrote the other book.

1. Craig Rice

_____ **A.** *Trial by Fury*

_____ **B.** *Home Sweet Homicide*

_____ **C.** *Grave Affair*

_____ **D.** *My Kingdom for a Hearse*

2. Charlotte Armstrong

_____ **A.** *Chocolate Cobweb*

_____ **B.** *Dram of Poison*

_____ **C.** *The Better to Eat You*

_____ **D.** *The Poisoned Chocolates Case*

3. Erle Stanley Gardner

_____ **A.** *The Case of the Seven Sneezes*

_____ **B.** *The Case of the Amorous Aunt*

_____ **C.** *The Case of the Demure Defendant*

_____ **D.** *The Case of the Fan-Dancer's Horse*

4. John Rhode

_____ **A.** *Death of an Artist*

_____ **B.** *Death of an Author*

_____ **C.** *Death of a Worldly Woman*

_____ **D.** *Death of a Bridegroom*

5. D. B. Olson

_____ **A.** *Death Walks on Cat Feet*

_____ **B.** *Cat and Mouse*

_____ **C.** *The Cat Wears a Mask*

_____ **D.** *The Cat Saw Murder*

6. Frances Crane

_____ **A.** *Applegreen Cat*

_____ **B.** *Turquoise Shop*

_____ **C.** *Black Alibi*

_____ **D.** *Yellow Violet*

7. Sara Woods

_____ **A.** *Enter Certain Murderers*

_____ **B.** *Serpent's Tooth*

_____ **C.** *The Evil That Men Do*

_____ **D.** *And Shame the Devil*

8. Kyle Hunt

_____ **A.** *Dead as a Dinosaur*

_____ **B.** *Sly as a Serpent*

_____ **C.** *Cruel as a Cat*

_____ **D.** *Cunning as a Fox*

9. Patrick Quentin

_____ **A.** *Puzzle for Inspector West*

_____ **B.** *Puzzle for Fiends*

_____ **C.** *Puzzle for Puppets*

_____ **D.** *Puzzle for Wantons*

10. Robert Bloch

_____ **A.** *Psycho*

_____ **B.** *Terror*

_____ **C.** *Firebug*

_____ **D.** *Chill*

WHAT'S IN A NAME?

We took the liberty of rewriting some of our favorite mystery fiction titles. Next to each of the authors listed below is our reworked title. Supply the real title and score 5 points for each correct answer.

1. Rex Stout, *Spoiled Broth*

_____

2. Michael Innes, *Evening of Mistakes*

_____

3. Ngaio Marsh, *A Bunch of Cops*

_____

4. Frances and Richard Lockridge, *Lengthy Bag of Bones*

_____

5. Sara Woods, *The Roguish Corvidae*

_____

6. Brett Halliday, *Murdering Maiden*

_____

7. June Thomson, *The Nun's Garb of Amorousness*

_____

8. William Irish, *The Armageddon Rock*

_____

9. George Harmon Coxe, *Thou Shalt Not Covet Thy Neighbor's Goods*

_____

10. Fredric Brown, *Last Call*

_____

11. E. W. Hornung, *March 15th*

_____

12. Dorothy Uhnak, *Fish Food*

_____

THE SIGN OF THE EIGHT

If you could save only a dozen whodunits, which ones would you choose?

A number of editors have attempted to answer that question by publishing series of noteworthy or memorable mystery novels. The various series are identifiable by a cover symbol or logo, and sometimes special identification markings on the back of the book. Score 5 points for each symbol you recognize.

1

2

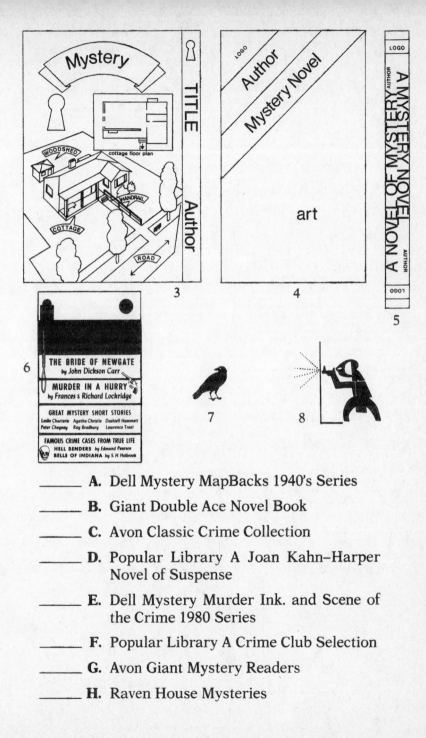

3 4 5

6

7 8

_____ **A.** Dell Mystery MapBacks 1940's Series

_____ **B.** Giant Double Ace Novel Book

_____ **C.** Avon Classic Crime Collection

_____ **D.** Popular Library A Joan Kahn–Harper Novel of Suspense

_____ **E.** Dell Mystery Murder Ink. and Scene of the Crime 1980 Series

_____ **F.** Popular Library A Crime Club Selection

_____ **G.** Avon Giant Mystery Readers

_____ **H.** Raven House Mysteries

SCORING

Read All About It!	_____
HIDDENHEREARE	
** BOTHGOODANDDBADGUYS**	_____
Leave 'Em Laughing	_____
Tall Tales	_____
Spot the Red Herring	_____
What's in a Name	_____
The Sign of the Eight	_____
** Chapter Total Score**	_____

The Verdict

If you scored between 338 and 247   You came through without a scratch.

If you scored between 246 and 123   You're bloodied but unbowed.

If you scored between 122 and 0   You're mortally wounded.

SOLUTIONS

Aha! We caught you looking! Finish that quiz all the way through before you look at these answers.

The great thing about seeing the answers to the questions in this book is that you can learn a lot about mysteries. One of our hopes in doing this book is that we'll lead people to discover new authors, new detectives, and new areas of the big world of mystery.

And by the way, we hope you did well on the quizzes.

POTPOURRI

Authors and Titles
1. D	2. E	3. A	4. B	5. C

Mystery Minutiae
1. C	2. C	3. D	4. C	5. B
6. C	7. A	8. C	9. D	10. C

Authors and Their Characters
1. F	2. H	3. A	4. J	5. B
6. I	7. D	8. C	9. E	10. G

Don't Buy a Book by its Cover
1. J	2. I	3. H	4. G	5. F
6. E	7. D	8. C	9. B	10. A

Free Associations
1. C	2. E	3. G	4. J	5. I
6. D	7. H	8. F	9. A	10. B

Elementary Questions
1. B	**2.** C	**3.** B	**4.** A	**5.** F
6. B	**7.** B	**8.** B	**9.** C	**10.** D
11. C	**12.** A	**13.** C	**14.** D	**15.** B
16. C	**17.** B	**18.** True. Cooking the mushrooms		

will not make them less toxic.   **19.** True   **20.** False

Just the Facts, Ma'am
1. *The Maltese Falcon*
2. Travis McGee
3. The Edgar Allan Poe Award (Edgars), a raven (what else?) statuette.
4. Ellery Queen, the Saint, and Nero Wolfe are all correct.
5. Alfred, Lord Tennyson
6. Sherlock Holmes
7. Henry Tibbett
8. Hildegarde Withers
9. Holmes had no smarter, younger brother (at least none known to Arthur Conan Doyle).
10. *An American Tragedy*

Telling Details
1. D	**2.** A	**3.** C	**4.** A	**5.** B
6. A	**7.** B	**8.** C	**9.** D	**10.** A

The Lingo
We gratefully acknowledge the assistance of the Glossaries included in *Murder Inc.*, edited by Dilys Wynn, Workman, NY, NY (1977), for this quiz.

1. I (A)	**2.** K (A)	**3.** P (B)	**4.** E (B)	**5.** A (A)
6. L (A)	**7.** J (A)	**8.** H (B)	**9.** C (B)	**10.** 2

(B—from Woman Police Constable?)   **11.** G (B)

12. Q (A)   **13.** O (A)   **14.** R (B—the American version
15. M (A)   **16.** D (A)   is a fence)
17. F (A)   **18.** N (B)

A Few Cross Words

1 D	O	2 R	O	3 T	H	Y	4 L	S	5 A	Y	E	R	6 S
E		A		O			I		R				I
7 L	I	F	E	R			8 N	O	T	H	9 I	N	G
L		F		10 T	H	11 U	G		I		N		N
12 S	A	L	E	S			13 N	A	B	S			O
H		E		14 T			L		15 T	16 H	I	17 E	F
18 A	M	S	19 T	E	R	D	A	M	20 M		E	21 A	T
N		I		E			22 C	O	D	F	23 I	S	H
24 N	A	25 M	E		N		O		26 T	A	T	E	E
O		C		27 I	T		28 D	O	N		G		F
N		29 K	O		30 S	31 E	E		32 L	O	B	O	U
		E				A	33 O	34 D	E				U
35 T	H	E	I	V	O	R	Y	D	A	G	G	E	R

ABOUT THE GOOD GUYS

Fitting the Description

1. D	**2.** F	**3.** K	**4.** I	**5.** G
6. B	**7.** L	**8.** E	**9.** C	**10.** H
11. A	**12.** J			

Supersleuths

1. B	**2.** A	**3.** B	**4.** A	**5.** C
6. A	**7.** C	**8.** B	**9.** C	**10.** D
11. C	**12.** A	**13.** C	**14.** D	**15.** A

It's a Living
1. A	**2.** A	**3.** P	**4.** A	**5.** P
6. A	**7.** P	**8.** P	**9.** P	**10.** A
11. A	**12.** P	**13.** A	**14.** A	**15.** P
16. A	**17.** P	**18.** P	**19.** P	**20.** P

British and Americans
1. B	**2.** A	**3.** A	**4.** B	**5.** A
6. B	**7.** B	**8.** B	**9.** A	**10.** A

Accessories
1. F   **2.** C   **3.** J   **4.** I   **5.** H
6. G (Philip Youngman Carter was the husband and literary adviser of Margery Allingham. Carter completed *Cargo of Eagles,* the book Allingham was writing prior to her death, and later wrote two more Albert Campion mysteries.)   **7.** E
8. A   **9.** B   **10.** D

More Minutiae
1. A	**2.** B	**3.** D	**4.** B	**5.** A
6. D	**7.** A	**8.** C	**9.** B	**10.** C
11. A	**12.** B	**13.** C	**14.** C	**15.** A
16. B	**17.** D	**18.** C	**19.** A	**20.** D

Admissible Evidence
1. H	**2.** E	**3.** A	**4.** J	**5.** B
6. C	**7.** D	**8.** G	**9.** F	**10.** I

Great Gumshoes
1. A	**2.** A	**3.** D	**4.** B	**5.** C
6. D	**7.** A	**8.** B	**9.** D	**10.** C

The Truth Will Out
1. T (but dozens of movies followed this last written work)
2. T	**3.** F	**4.** F	**5.** T	**6.** F
7. T	**8.** T	**9.** F	**10.** T	**11.** F
12. F	**13.** T	**14.** T	**15.** F (It's Gay.)	

MORE THAN JUST FRIENDS— MEET THE SIDEKICKS

"Watson . . . "

1. I	**2.** A	**3.** G	**4.** B	**5.** F
6. E	**7.** J	**8.** C	**9.** H	**10.** D

Unlikely Partnerships

1. C	**2.** C	**3.** A	**4.** B	**5.** D
6. D	**7.** C	**8.** A	**9.** C	**10.** D

Working with Them or Against Them

1. F	**2.** J	**3.** H	**4.** A	**5.** I
6. B	**7.** C	**8.** G	**9.** D	**10.** E

MUCH MORE THAN JUST FRIENDS— WIVES AND LOVERS

His and Hers

1. F	**2.** C	**3.** E	**4.** D	**5.** I
6. J	**7.** B	**8.** G	**9.** H	**10.** A

The Better Half

1. A	**2.** C	**3.** B	**4.** A	**5.** C
6. B	**7.** B	**8.** A	**9.** A	**10.** B
11. D	**12.** D	**13.** A	**14.** A	**15.** C

Just Friends?

1. M	**2.** M	**3.** D	**4.** W	**5.** S
6. S	**7.** S	**8.** M	**9.** W	**10.** S

Couples and Their Origins

1. D ii   **2.** B iv   **3.** E iii   **4.** A v   **5.** C i
(Georgia, an explorer, who is not usually detecting, is the principal sleuth in this spy thriller.)

WHERE?

Travelers or Homebodies?
1. T	**2.** H	**3.** H	**4.** T	**5.** T
6. H	**7.** H	**8.** T	**9.** T	**10.** H
11. T	**12.** T	**13.** T	**14.** H	**15.** T

The Detective At Home
1. C	**2.** D	**3.** A	**4.** B	**5.** D
6. A	**7.** C	**8.** B	**9.** A	**10.** C
11. C	**12.** C			

Where They Hang Their Hats
1. C	**2.** B	**3.** D	**4.** A	**5.** A
6. C	**7.** B	**8.** D	**9.** B	**10.** C

Hometowns
1. D	**2.** G	**3.** E	**4.** B	**5.** J
6. A	**7.** H	**8.** I	**9.** C	**10.** F

Foul Play
1. Archery or chess (Either is correct.)   **2.** Basketball
3. Horse racing   **4.** Football   **5.** Cricket   **6.** Golf
7. Tennis   **8.** Skiing   **9.** Cricket   **10.** Baseball
11. Tennis   **12.** Golf   **13.** Baseball

WHODUNIT AND WHY?

Fallen Arches
1. D	**2.** B	**3.** D	**4.** A	**5.** D
6. B	**7.** A	**8.** D (In later books Trent reforms		

and is a good guy.)   **9.** C   **10.** B

Eyewitness Accounts
1. A	**2.** C	**3.** D	**4.** B

Whydunits
1. F	**2.** T	**3.** F	**4.** F	**5.** F
6. T	**7.** F	**8.** T	**9.** T	**10.** F

Classic Cases
1. C	**2.** B	**3.** B	**4.** D	**5.** D
6. B	**7.** C	**8.** A	**9.** B	**10.** B
11. D	**12.** B	**13.** D	**14.** A	**15.** A

Eternal Nemeses
1. E	**2.** F	**3.** D	**4.** A	**5.** C
6. B				

DICKS OF THE FLICKS

Crime on the Silver Screen
1. B	**2.** C	**3.** G	**4.** E	**5.** B
6. A and C	**7.** D	**8.** C	**9.** A	**10.** B
11. D	**12.** B	**13.** C	**14.** D	**15.** D
16. A, B, D	**17.** D	**18.** A and D	**19.** D	
20. A, B, C				

Chandler on Film
1. B and D **2.** A and E **3.** C

The Barrymore Gang
1. E	**2.** L and J	**3.** J	**4.** E	**5.** E
6. L	**7.** J	**8.** L	**9.** E	**10.** E

Grant's Leading Ladies
1. D	**2.** A	**3.** E	**4.** B	**5.** C

Actors in Series
1. F	**2.** D	**3.** A	**4.** I	**5.** G
6. E	**7.** C	**8.** J	**9.** B	**10.** H

Modus Operandi
1. C   **2.** D   **3.** A   **4.** F   **5.** B
6. E

Femme Fatales
1. B   **2.** D   **3.** E   **4.** F   **5.** C
6. A

Death at 32 Frames per Second
1. D   **2.** A   **3.** C   **4.** B   **5.** A
6. D   **7.** B   **8.** C

A Title Spelled "B-O-X O-F-F-I-C-E"
1. F   **2.** E   **3.** L   **4.** J   **5.** H
6. G   **7.** K   **8.** A   **9.** I   **10.** B
11. D   **12.** C

Leading Men and Women
1. E   **2.** A, B, and C   **3.** A, B
4. A, B, and E   **5.** B and C   **6.** B
7. A and D   **8.** B, D, and E   **9.** B and C
10. A, D, and E   **11.** E   **12.** A, D, and E
13. A and D   **14.** E   **15.** E
16. A, C, and D   **17.** A, B, and D   **18.** C and D
19. B, C, D, and E   **20.** C and E   **21.** D and E
22. B and C   **23.** A, D, and E   **24.** A, B, C, and D
25. A, B, C, D, and E **26.** C   **27.** B, C, and D
28. A, C, D, and E   **29.** A and B   **30.** D

It Can Only Be . . .
1. D   **2.** G   **3.** H   **4.** B   **5.** F
6. A   **7.** C   **8.** J   **9.** I   **10.** E

COPS ON THE BOX

Murder in Your Living Room
1. A	**2.** C	**3.** D	**4.** B	**5.** C
6. D	**7.** D	**8.** A	**9.** C	**10.** B
11. B	**12.** A	**13.** D	**14.** C	**15.** D
16. A	**17.** C			

Cops or PI's
1. P	**2.** P	**3.** C	**4.** C	**5.** P
6. C	**7.** P	**8.** C	**9.** P	**10.** P

Professions
1. C and E **2.** A   **3.** B and D **4.** F

Murder, U.S.A.
1. I	**2.** E	**3.** G	**4.** B and F	**5.** D and H
6. C	**7.** A	**8.** J		

Great Mystery Series
1. F	**2.** I	**3.** A	**4.** G	**5.** C
6. B	**7.** H	**8.** D	**9.** E	**10.** J

The Facts of the Matter
1. F (It was the piano.)   **2.** T (J.R. is Barnaby's cousin.)
3. F (It's Joe.)   **4.** F (They worked with Captain Greer of
The Mod Squad.)   **5.** F (It's Michael.)   **6.** T   **7.** T
8. F (It was Phyllis Kirk.)   **9.** F (They protect *The Streets
of San Francisco*.)   **10.** F (It was Chicago.)

The Mostest
1. C	**2.** E	**3.** A	**4.** B	**5.** D

Well Off or Hard Up?
1. W   2. H   3. W   4. W   5. W
6. H   7. H   8. H   9. H   10. W

LITTLE-KNOWN FACTS ABOUT THE AUTHORS

By Night, a Mystery Writer. By Day . . .
1. A   2. D   3. A   4. B   5. A
6. A   7. C   8. C   9. A   10. B
11. A   12. C

Pseudonyms and Aliases
1. B   2. D   3. A   4. C (Carr created locked-room-puzzle solver Gideon Fell; Carter Dickson was the pen name for the creator of Sir Henry Merrivale. Carr/Dickson is also known as Carr Dickson.)   5. E   6. G   7. F   8. J
9. H   10. I ("Ellery Queen" is a pseudonym for Manfred B. Lee and Frederick Dannay.)

Telltale Paragraphs
1. D   2. B   3. D   4. A   5. C

John D. MacDonald— Showing His True Colors
1. F   2. H   3. D   4. L   5. C
6. I   7. G   8. K   9. J   10. B
11. A   12. E

Eight By-the-Way By-lines
1. C   2. B   3. C   4. D
5. D   6. A   7. B   8. C

MISCELLANEOUS MAYHEM

Read All About It!

1. I	**2.** H	**3.** M	**4.** U	**5.** P
6. G	**7.** V	**8.** C	**9.** T	**10.** Q
11. B	**12.** K	**13.** L	**14.** A	**15.** N
16. F	**17.** E	**18.** O	**19.** J	**20.** D
21. S	**22.** R			

Hiddenherearethegoodandbadguys

```
H I D D E N H E R E A R E B O T H G O O D A N D B A D G U Y S
M B C E A H L A C X S R V E B A T H N Q U A I N R U E V B C A
C J U F P G R W N K O P U N E X J O S E D A S I L V A M F S T
O A J E B A A E C A D O Y C I M R T E B L R C T O M N U I C U
L N X L C H R F I L U R G O L J E E W R M O R I A R T Y N E R
D R A B I A L T L X V D F L A M B E A U P V E H S B E A Y T N
R V C R U M I O M U Y B D I G L K Z R Q B E H R E N S R P X I
Y A L C J B E R A E N B O N A P A R T E E G J V C U S C E S N
N R A E A L G N I S N A A N L E R X J O A Q U I N H A W K S J
S E N R N E B S P E C T R E R E L D L N O B C L P D F L N J N
T V Y D C D U J L E V E Z M V I A U T D N S C O E B H P A U A
E Q A R Z O K Q E R S B E R T R A M L Y N C H R T R B H E D O
M A R T I N B E C K J P B H U B G E F A T H M N E C O Y L G P
Y C D S S P B L O F E L D A M E L O G D U A I R R G L U D E S
L W C I S A F W Q M V E O C O C K R I L L F Q U S D O V X D T
A L N C A R L V O N G R O O T E L C A Y V I M M O I F D S E M
I N T E R N A T I O N A L C O P S C R O O K S A N D S P I E S
```

Leave 'Em Laughing
1. D	**2.** B	**3.** C	**4.** A	**5.** C
6. B	**7.** A	**8.** C	**9.** C	**10.** D

Tall Tales
1. D **2.** H **3.** J **4.** F (the case that introduced TV's Lieutenant Columbo) **5.** I

Spot the Red Herring

1. C. Shelley Smith

2. D. Anthony Berkeley

3. A. Anthony Boucher

4. C. A. B. Cunningham

5. B. John Creasey and Christianna Brand are both correct — they each wrote a book with that title.

6. C. Cornell Woolrich

7. C. Hugh Pentecost AKA Judson Philips[1]

8. A. Frances and Richard Lockridge

9. A. John Creasey

10. D. Ross Macdonald

What's in a Name

1. *Too Many Cooks*

2. *Night of Errors*

3. *A Clutch of Constables*

4. *Long Skeleton*

5. *The Knavish Crow*

6. *Homicidal Virgin*

7. *The Habit of Loving*

8. *The Doom Stone*

9. *The Last Commandment*

10. *One for the Road*

11. *The Ides of March*

12. *Bait*

The Sign of the Eight

1. E   2. D   3. A   4. C   5. B

6. G   7. H   8. F

FOOTPRINT

[1] All the titles in question 7 come from Shakespeare's plays.

FINAL SCORING

Potpourri   _____

About the Good Buys   _____

More than Just Friends   _____

Much More than Just Friends   _____

Where?   _____

Whodunit and Why?   _____

Dicks of the Flicks   _____

Cops on the Box   _____

Little-known Facts About the
    Authors   _____

Miscellaneous Mayhem   _____

    Book Total Score   _____

The Final Verdict

There is a total of 2,806 points in this quiz book. How did you do?

If you scored between 2,806 and 2,201 points

You are to be congratulated. You are a Master Sleuth and are ready for the Post-mortem Quiz.

2,200 and 1,791 points

With a few more cases under your belt, you, too, could be a Master Sleuth. Try the Postmortem Quiz—if you dare.

1,790 and 1,309 points

You are on the right track. Check with Archie Goodwin or Paul Drake. They'll point the way.

1,308 and 735 points

You are sentenced to one mystery a night for an indeterminate and most pleasurable time.

734 and 0 points

Put this in the mail to Aunt Agnes. Maybe she can do better.

POSTMORTEM —

A MASTER

SLEUTH'S QUIZ

Do you feel an uncomfortable heat in the pit of your stomach . . . And a nasty thumping at the top of your head? I call it detective fever.

— WILKIE COLLINS, *The Moonstone*

You may find the following questions very difficult. We did. That's why we've saved them for the end. Score 3 points for each correct answer.

Match the titles and authors.

_____ 1. *One Minute Past Eight*

_____ 2. *Two in the Bush*

_____ 3. *Five Pieces of Jade*

_____ 4. *Eleven Came Back*

A. Mabel Seeley

B. John Ball

C. George Bagby

D. George Harmon Coxe

Match the titles and correct authors.

_____	**1.** *Death Demands an Audience*	**A.** Alfred Tack
_____	**2.** *Curtain Call for a Corpse*	**B.** William Cox
_____	**3.** *A Murder Is Staged*	**C.** Helen Reilly
_____	**4.** *Death on Location*	**D.** Thomas A. Plummer
_____	**5.** *Death Haunts the Repertory*	**E.** Josephine Bell

Identify the book written by each author.

1. Kenneth Fearing

_____ **A.** *The Clocks*

_____ **B.** *The Skeleton in the Clock*

_____ **C.** *The Clock Strikes Twelve*

_____ **D.** *The Big Clock*

2. Ed McBain

_____ **A.** *Lemon in the Basket*

_____ **B.** *Sour Cream with Everything*

_____ **C.** *Bread*

_____ **D.** *The Proof of the Pudding*

3. G. K. Chesterton

_____ **A.** *The Thin Man*

_____ **B.** *The Man Who Was Thursday*

_____ **C.** *The Man in the Brown Suit*

_____ **D.** *The Man Who Came to Dinner*

4. Dell Shannon

_____ **A.** *Deuces Wild*

_____ **B.** *Mr. Moto's Three Aces*

_____ **C.** *Casino Royale*

_____ **D.** *The Man Who Held Five Aces*

Match the authors with their books.

_____ **1.** Agatha Christie   **A.** *The Judas Cat*

_____ **2.** Nicholas Freeling   **B.** *Cat of Many Tails*

_____ **3.** Ellery Queen   **C.** *Cats Prowl at Night*

_____ **4.** Dorothy Salisbury Davis   **D.** *The Cat Saw Murder*

_____ **5.** Erle Stanley Gardner   **E.** *Cat Among the Pigeons*

_____ **6.** Dolores B. Olsen   **F.** *Because of the Cats*

Identify the book written by each author.

1. Margery Allingham

_____ **A.** *The Blue Room*

_____ **B.** *A Flash of Green*

_____ **C.** *A Study in Scarlet*

_____ **D.** *Black Plumes*

2. Julian Symons

_____ **A.** *Money on Murder*

_____ **B.** *The Price of Murder*

_____ **C.** *The Broken Penny*

_____ **D.** *The Far Side of the Dollar*

3. Hammond Innes

_____ **A.** *Gale Warnings*

_____ **B.** *Stormy Night*

_____ **C.** *Rain Before Seven*

_____ **D.** *Typhoon's Secret*

4. Charlotte Armstrong

_____ **A.** *The Case of the Gilded Lily*

_____ **B.** *The Case of the Constant Suicides*

_____ **C.** *The Case of the Weird Sisters*

_____ **D.** *The Case of Sonya Weyward*

5. Harry Longbough

_____ **A.** *Lady in a Cage*

_____ **B.** *No Way to Treat a Lady*

_____ **C.** *The Phantom Lady*

_____ **D.** *The Lady in the Lake*

6. Joan Fleming

_____ **A.** *The Five Red Herrings*

_____ **B.** *Killer Dolphin*

_____ **C.** *Death of a Sardine*

_____ **D.** *The Cape Cod Mystery*

7. Dorothy B. Hughes

_____ **A.** *Ride the Pink Horse*

_____ **B.** *Tiger in the Smoke*

_____ **C.** *Elephants Can Remember*

_____ **D.** *The Zebra Striped Hearse*

8. William Irish

_____ **A.** *The Waltz of Death*

_____ **B.** *The Dancing Detective*

_____ **C.** *Death and the Dancing Footman*

_____ **D.** *Dancers in Mourning*

9. Doris Miles Disney

_____ **A.** *Daughter of Time*

_____ **B.** *The Husband*

_____ **C.** *Mother Hunt*

_____ **D.** *The Magic Grandfather*

10. Jean Potts

_____ **A.** *Thirteen White Tulips*

_____ **B.** *Black Orchids*

_____ **C.** *The Daffodil Affair*

_____ **D.** *Go, Lovely Rose*

Match the detectives with their creators.

_____ **1.** Father Dowling

_____ **2.** Soeur Angèle

_____ **3.** Brother Cadfael

_____ **4.** Reverend Martin Buell

_____ **5.** Father Koesler

A. Margaret Scherf

B. Ellis Peters

C. William Kienzle

D. Ralph McInerny

E. Henri Catalan

Match the titles with their authors.

I

_____	**1.** *The Religious Body*	**A.**	Tony Hillirman
_____	**2.** *Quiet as a Nun*	**B.**	Catharine Aird
_____	**3.** *The Blessing Way*	**C.**	Dorothy Gilman
_____	**4.** *Nun in the Closet*	**D.**	Antonia Fraser
_____	**5.** *Unbecoming Habits*	**E.**	Tim Heald

II

_____	**1.** *Murder at Cambridge*	**A.**	Quentin Patrick
_____	**2.** *Harvard Has a Murder*	**B.**	M. R. Hodgin
		C.	Miles Burton
_____	**3.** *Qbsequies at Oxford*	**D.**	Timothy Fuller
_____	**4.** *Murder Out of School*	**E.**	Janet Caird
_____	**5.** *The Student Body*	**F.**	Edmond Crispin
_____	**6.** *Murder Scholastic*		

III

_____	**1.** *The Eyes at the Window*	**A.**	Ernest Bramah
		B.	George Selmark
_____	**2.** *Eyes That Watch You*	**C.**	Laurence Lariar
_____	**3.** *The Eyes of Max Carrados*	**D.**	Nick Carter
_____	**4.** *The Eyes of the Tiger*	**E.**	George Hopley
_____	**5.** *The Eyes Around Me*	**F.**	Gavin Black
_____	**6.** *The Girl with the Frightened Eyes*		

IV

_____ 1. *Two-Thirds of a Ghost*

_____ 2. *Three-Thirds of a Ghost*

_____ 3. *Tomorrow's Ghost*

_____ 4. *The Ghost It Was*

_____ 5. *Too Many Ghosts*

_____ 6. *Ghost of a Chance*

A. Richard Hull

B. Helen McCloy

C. Anthony Price

D. Frank Usher

E. Timothy Fuller

F. Paul Gallico

V

_____ 1. *Uncle Silas*

_____ 2. *Alias Uncle Hugo*

_____ 3. *Uncle Abner*

_____ 4. *Death of His Uncle*

_____ 5. *Uncle Paul*

_____ 6. *Let's Kill Uncle*

A. Melville D. Post

B. C. H. B. Kitchen

C. Rohan O'Grady

D. Manning Coles

E. Celia Fremlin

F. Sheridan LeFanu

VI

_____ 1. *Death Is Late to Lunch*

_____ 2. *Meat for Murder*

_____ 3. *The Chocolate Mousse Murders*

_____ 4. *Someone Is Killing the Great Chefs of Europe*

_____ 5. *Inspector Ghote Breaks an Egg*

_____ 6. *Dine and Be Dead*

A. Fred Halliday

B. Gwendoline Butler

C. H. R. Keating

D. Lange Lewis

E. Nan and Ivan Lyons

F. Theodora DuBois

VII

_____ 1. *Painted for the Kill*   A. Lucy Cores

_____ 2. *Fatal in My*   B. Brian Cleeve
        Fashion
                                     C. Robert Kyle
_____ 3. *Death of a Painted*
        Lady   D. Patricia McGerr

                                     E. Margery Allingham
_____ 4. *Fashion in Shrouds*

_____ 5. *Model for Murder*

VIII

_____ 1. *Doll*   A. Ed McBain

_____ 2. *Hanno's Doll*   B. Brett Halliday

_____ 3. *Death of a Doll*   C. Evelyn Piper

_____ 4. *Dolls Are Deadly*   D. Algernon
                                        Blackwood
_____ 5. *The Doll and One*
        Other   E. Hilda Lawrence

IX

_____ 1. *Wolf, Wolf*   A. R. A. Freeman

_____ 2. *The Lone Wolf*   B. Josephine Bell

_____ 3. *Wolves of the Sea*   C. Manning Lee
                                        Stokes
_____ 4. *Wolf Howls Murder*
                                     D. Mignon G.
_____ 5. *Wolf in Man's*   Eberhart
        Clothing
                                     E. Gaston LeRoux
_____ 6. *The Shadow of the*
        Wolf   F. Louis Vance

X

_____ 1. *Puzzle in Pewter*   **A.** Michael Collins

_____ 2. *Iron Clew*   **B.** Elizabeth Gresham

_____ 3. *The Brass Rainbow*   **C.** Donald Hamilton

_____ 4. *The Copper Box*   **D.** J. S. Fletcher

_____ 5. *The Steel Mirror*   **E.** William LeQueux

_____ 6. *Behind the Bronze*   **F.** Alice Tilton
      Door

XI

_____ 1. *The Widow*   **A.** Nicholas Freeling
      LeRouge

                       B. Margot Bennett

_____ 2. *Widows Wear*   **C.** Elizabeth Sanxay
      Weeds   Holding

_____ 3. *The Widow*   **D.** Emile Gaboriau

_____ 4. *Widow's Mite*   **E.** A. A. Fair

_____ 5. *The Widow of Bath*

XII

_____ 1. *Detection of Dr.*   **A.** Clemence Dane
      Sam Johnson

                       B. Jack Finney

_____ 2. *Re-Enter Sir John*   **C.** James M. Cain

_____ 3. *Someone from the*   **D.** Lillian De La Torre
      Past

                       E. Margot Bennett

_____ 4. *Time and Again*

_____ 5. *Past All Dishonor*

XIII

_____	1. *Suffer a Witch*	**A.**	E. X. Ferrars
_____	2. *Witch Miss Seeton*	**B.**	Heron Carvic
_____	3. *Witch of the Low Tide*	**C.**	Rae Foley
		D.	John Dickson Carr
_____	4. *Alibi for a Witch*	**E.**	Paula Allardyce (AKA Charity Blackstock)
_____	5. *Witch's Sabbath*		

XIV

_____	1. *Sheep May Safely Graze*	**A.**	F. H. Hall
_____	2. *Hanged for a Sheep*	**B.**	Simon Harvester
_____	3. *Black Sheep, White Sheep*	**C.**	Rosemary Gatenby
_____	4. *In the White Lamb Days*	**D.**	Dorothy S. Davis
_____	5. *Lamb to the Slaughter*	**E.**	Dorothy Eden

SOLUTIONS

1. D	2. C	3. B	4. A	
1. C	2. E	3. A	4. B	5. D
1. D	2. C	3. B	4. A	
1. E	2. F	3. B	4. A	5. C
6. D				
1. D	2. C	3. A	4. C	5. B
6. C	7. A	8. B	9. D	10. D

1. D   2. E   3. B   4. A   5. C

I

1. B   2. D   3. A   4. C   5. E

II

1. A   2. D   3. F   4. C   5. B
6. E

III

1. B   2. E   3. A   4. D   5. F
6. C

IV

1. B   2. E   3. C   4. A   5. D
6. F

V

1. F   2. D   3. A   4. B   5. E
6. C

VI

1. F   2. D   3. A   4. E   5. C
6. B

VII

1. A   2. D   3. B   4. E   5. C

VIII

1. A   2. C   3. E   4. B   5. D

IX

1. B   **2.** F   **3.** E   **4.** C   **5.** D
6. A

X

1. B   **2.** F   **3.** A   **4.** D   **5.** C
6. E

XI

1. D   **2.** E   **3.** A   **4.** C   **5.** B

XII

1. D   **2.** A   **3.** E   **4.** B   **5.** C

XIII

1. C   **2.** B   **3.** D   **4.** A   **5.** E

XIV

1. B   **2.** C   **3.** D   **4.** A   **5.** E

SCORING

Postmortem ————

The Verdict

If you scored between 333 and 210

Simply remarkable. We congratulate you.

If you scored between 209 and 91

You can walk past the nearest police station with your head held high.

If you scored between 90 and 0

You have a love of mysteries and a great wealth of authors and books to read. What more can you ask for?